DARE TO BE A
DIFFERENCE
Maker
Volume 7

DARE TO BE A
DIFFERENCE
Maker
Volume 7

DIFFERENCE MAKERS WHO DARE TO LIVE
WITH PASSION, FOLLOW THEIR PURPOSE
AND COMMIT TO HELPING OTHERS!

MICHELLE PRINCE

Dedication

To all the "Difference Makers" in the world
who are making a difference by following your heart.
Thanks for letting your "light" shine!

Introduction

For many years as I worked in "Corporate America" I would say to myself, "I just want to make a difference!" I was selling software and I'm sure I was making some difference for my clients but not in the way I wanted to. I wanted to help, serve, encourage and motivate people. I wanted to make a positive impact on their lives but I didn't know how...how could just one person really make a significant difference? So I didn't...for a long time. I continued to work in an area that wasn't my passion or calling. I didn't follow my heart and God's promptings to go in the direction of my purpose and dreams. Instead, I just let year after year go by feeling unfulfilled, unhappy, and spiritually broken.

That is, until one day in 2008 when I had my "aha" moment. It hit me like a ton of bricks that it's my responsibility to follow my passions and purpose. No one can do that for me. I took action to write my first book, *Winning In Life Now*, began to speak, motivate and mentor others to live their best life and, as they say, "the rest is history."

What I found over this journey is that we all have a desire to make a difference. We all want to live with passion and follow our God-given callings; our purpose. It's through this understanding that I decided to write this series of books.

Dare To Be A Difference Maker 6 is my vision to have a unique collection of narratives, not only from inspired leaders, but also from those I see making a difference and impacting others in their everyday personal and professional life. These stories are about *real* people who are making a *real* difference, even on a small scale.

My mission in creating the "Difference Maker Movement" and in writing the series of *Dare To Be A Difference Maker* books is that you will gain inspiration, wisdom, and the courage you need in order to get through life's tough challenges and make a difference for others in the process.

So many people I speak with these days discuss their issues as though they are losing hope. It is my vision for this book to reach the masses and have a powerful effect on people in their everyday lives. It is my prayer that this book, and all the volumes, will breathe new life into your mind and spirit and that it will inspire you to take action in order to help others.

I've selected an exclusive group of difference-makers who I know can motivate, inspire, and be a part of a movement to change people's lives. Everyone can do this; it just takes commitment and honoring of our unique and sacred gifts. It is to those people I dedicate this book.

From one "Difference Maker" to another,

Michelle

P.S. Do you or anyone you know have a story about making a difference? We are currently interviewing authors for our next book and would love to have you join us in this amazing journey. To submit an entry, please contact Info@PrincePerformance.com for more details. While one powerful story can be fascinating many can move mountains!

Table of Contents

1

My Buddy!
An Angel Passing Through
Ellen Arnott

Have you ever felt that an angel was watching over you? Sometimes we are fortunate to encounter an angel during our own lifetime, just passing through. When we are blessed to encounter one, we need to tell the story.

This is the story of my youngest brother, Chuckie, as I remember him. Chuckie was never a burden and was a wonderful addition to our family. He brought much joy to Mom, Dad, and all of his brothers and sisters. In his brief six years, he made an impact on all of our lives by demonstrating unconditional love, compassion, and empathy with everyone.

I was almost ten years old when my brother, Chuckie, was born in 1955. He was a beautiful baby boy with blonde hair and big blue eyes. The doctors told Mom and Dad that Chuckie had Down Syndrome and explained the limitations that would bring.

One doctor told Mom that Chuckie needed to be put in an institution because he would bring hardships and people would look down on the whole family. Mom could not believe what this doctor was saying. She told the doctor that Chuckie was her child, and he would not be put in an institution.

Growing up with Chuckie ("Buddy")

My brother Bobby was two-and-a-half years old when Chuckie was born. He grew very close to Chuckie, and they often played together. Both of them delighted in playing with the little Matchbox cars that Bobby had accumulated. The two of them would sit for hours making the sound of motorcars, while they both pushed along their little cars on the kitchen floor. I can still hear those cars!

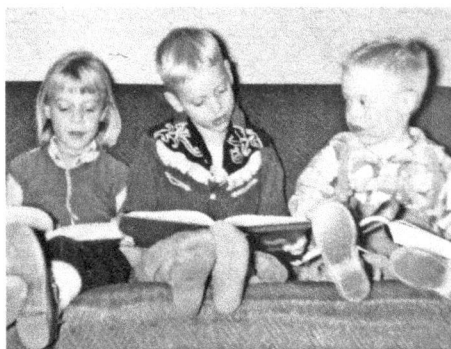

Pam, Bobby and Chuckie

It was Bobby who called Chuckie "Buddy," and the name stuck. After that, each one of us was "Buddy" to Chuckie. When anyone looked sad, Chuckie would put his precious little hand on their shoulder and lovingly say "Buddy" to remind them that they were his "Buddy."

My Buddy

More than once, when I was sad and crying, Chuckie would come into my bedroom, put his little hand on my shoulder, and with a sad face, say "Buddy." I immediately realized the love coming from within him. As soon as I smiled, he would give back a smile so big that it would melt anyone's heart.

Then he would give me a big hug. Chuckie shared his love for all of us with his hugs. Each time, it felt as though he was like a guardian angel watching over me, turning sadness into smiles.

Morning Visits

Chuckie typically woke up early each morning, with a very wet diaper. He would then crawl into bed with one of us—usually Carol. He seemed to know that Carol would get up right away and change his diaper. Once dry and comfortable, he would crawl in with Mom and Dad.

Other times, Chuckie would climb into his big brother Tom's bed. Chuckie would wait patiently for Tom's eyes to open. Tom would wake up to Chuckie's big blue eyes and a big smile. Chuckie then gave Tom one of his cars to play with, and he started making driving noises as he drove over the hills and valleys on his big brother's blanket.

Learning to Walk – by Pedaling and Pumping

Chuckie was slow to walk and talk, but we really did not realize there was anything different from other babies his age. He did not crawl. He more or less scooted on the floor, so we would play floor games with him. He also enjoyed trying to do floor exercises with Mom and "Jack Lalanne" on TV. Now that was a sight!

When Chuckie was between two and three years old, Mom and Dad won a tricycle and a pedal fire truck at the church's Fall Festival. Chuckie was not walking yet, so Mom started helping him learn to push the pedals on the tricycle with his feet. Mom would kneel down on the floor to hold his feet on the pedals as the tricycle moved along.

I remember helping Chuckie on the tricycle, and then one day he began to push the pedals himself. At first he moved very slowly. As he improved, he was moving all over the basement on the tricycle. One spring day, we took the tricycle outside. Off Chuckie went, up and down the driveway, smiling all the way.

With Chuckie's legs strengthened, and him walking, he was able to achieve the pumping motion needed to move the fire truck pedals. He loved his fire truck. He would go back and forth on the driveway for hours. He went on the street only one time. When told the road was only for big cars and not the fire trucks, he got it. He stayed off the street from that day forward.

Fun Outdoors in the Summertime

In the summertime, Chuckie would sit in the soft dirt on the side of the house and play with his cars. Still making his typical car motor sounds, he moved his cars along the imaginary dirt roads.

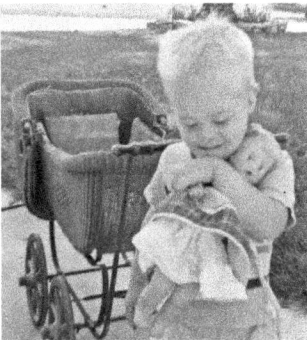

Chuckie loved his babies

One day, he found some baby dolls that I had outgrown, and he was thrilled. He would walk up and down the driveway pushing his baby dolls in a wicker doll carriage. He was delighted to hug and love them as if they were real babies.

Chuckie enjoyed the summertime when he could do so many things outside, including helping Dad or his big brother mow the lawn. He was up and eager to help with his own little lawn mower any time of the day.

He loved to swing and slide, too. Sisters Carol and Pam and brother Bob would race Chuckie to the swing set. Sometimes Carol would bend down low beside him pretending to be exhausted because she was running as fast as she could. They would giggle all the way. Chuckie could swing for what seemed like hours. Often Carol would come up with an enticing reason to go inside such as "Let's see what Mommy is doing," and then they would run back to the house.

We all enjoyed the longer summer days and playing outside in the backyard. Chuckie enjoyed picnics, outside games, or picking radishes, green beans, or better yet, strawberries from the garden. It was hard not to eat the strawberries as they were freshly picked. Chuckie managed to get his share.

Chuckie liked flying kites and playing ball games. He liked the rough and tumble games he played with Dad and the boys. Chuckie was tough, keeping up with his older brothers. He loved to run with the ball and roll on the ground when he was tackled, always laughing. In baseball, he would run wherever the ball would go until someone caught it. Chuckie was like an angel in the outfield.

Chuckie's Baby Sister

Chuckie was almost three when our sister Debi was born in December, 1957. He loved the new baby. He would bring her things and put them in her crib. Often he would sit next to Mom while she was feeding Debi and hug her whenever he could reach her. Debi still has fond memories of Chuckie's many special hugs.

A Little Helper? Lots of Dust and Ashes!

When Chuckie was about four, he watched Mom cleaning the basement fireplace. While Mom was busy cleaning the basement, Chuckie decided to go upstairs and help with the fireplace in the living room. He took the shovel by the fireplace and started scooping and flinging ashes out of the fireplace and into the living room. When Mom came upstairs, all she saw was what looked like smoke coming out of the living room, and she thought the house was on fire.

When she went into the living room, there was Chuckie still flinging the shovel full of ashes out into the living room. Chuckie was covered in soot—black hair and black face with his big blue eyes and a big accomplished smile on his face.

Chuckie thought he was helping clean out the fireplace ashes. Mom picked him up—with her extended arms—put him into the bathtub and started cleaning him up. Mom said it took three head washes, and she still didn't get him totally clean. By the time the rest of us came home from school, all was clean. We had no idea that the event even took place until Mom told us about her little helper and the ashes in the living room.

Precious Moments with Chuckie

Giggles would erupt when we blew on Chuckie's tummy, making a funny noise. Also, we "exchanged noses" (using the thumb between the index and third fingers) while tickling his tummy. He would laugh so hard that it became contagious. Everyone laughed until we could hardly breathe.

Birthday Cake!

Mealtime was never a problem with Chuckie. He enjoyed breakfast, lunch and dinner. His favorite food was Cocoa Puffs, which he preferred every morning. Add to that the chocolate-covered marshmallow cookies, which he asked for on a regular basis. To his credit, he was very patient and understood when it was too close to mealtime for snacks.

But birthdays were something he loved even more. It did not matter if it was his birthday or another's. Birthday parties were a favorite time for the whole family.

An Angel Among Us Falls Ill

When Chuckie was about five-and-a-half years old, Dad and the boys were playing football along with some neighbors when an accident occurred. A neighbor kicked a football about 7-10 yards right into Chuckie's abdomen.

Chuckie fell down breathless. Mom and Dad took him to the doctor who did not find anything wrong. However, within six weeks, it was apparent that Chuckie was not doing well. He was tired, listless, and not himself. Mom and Dad took him back to the doctor who arranged more tests. It was then that Chuckie was diagnosed with Acute Leukemia in October of 1960.

While Chuckie was sick, Carol would sometimes hear him whimper at night. She would go into his room, sit on his bed, and ask him what was wrong. He would say, "Legs hurt." So she would rub his legs until he would tell her, "Better," and then he would go back to sleep. No matter how sick Chuckie was, when asked, he would say "Better" in a soft, appreciative voice with his sweet loving smile. He never complained.

Illinois Research Hospital

Over several months, Chuckie had regular visits to the hospital for treatment. The treatments did seem to be helping him. He had more energy and seemed to be better until late summer 1961 when Chuckie was hospitalized.

Mom went every day to be with him. Dad dropped Mom off at the hospital on his way to work, and he took three-year-old Debi to work with him.

I became chief cook and bottle washer for my sisters and brothers—making meals, cleaning up, making and packing lunches, and getting everyone off to school. We all missed Chuckie and prayed for him to come home.

Confirmation

One day, a Catholic Bishop came to the hospital to visit the children who were considered terminal. If the child or family wanted the Blessing of Confirmation, the Bishop would provide it.

After the Bishop confirmed Chuckie, he said to Chuckie, "You are now a Soldier of Christ." With his sparkling blue eyes and big smile, Chuckie happily said to the Bishop, "Who, me?" The Bishop hugged Chuckie and said to Mom, "You have a beautiful boy here."

Clean Hands and Butterfly Kisses

Chuckie never liked to have his hands dirty. He would often ask any of us to help him clean his hands by showing us his dirty hands. One day a black nurse came in to check on Chuckie's IV site. Chuckie had never seen a black person before and he would not let her touch him, saying, "Dirty Hands." The nurse was so sweet and showed him the inside of her hands and Chuckie was satisfied.

She talked with Chuckie often and she was very patient with him. One day she asked Chuckie if he would like a "butterfly kiss" and he said "yes". She then batted her eyelashes gently on Chuckie's cheek. He was so delighted and giggled. Then before she left the room Chuckie gave the nurse a big hug and a kiss on her cheek.

Chuckie's Last Days - An Angel Passing Through

During his stay in the hospital, several of the doctors and nurses visited Chuckie. They complemented Mom and Dad on raising such a beautiful boy. One of the doctors gave Mom and Dad the bad news that Chuckie would not be with us much longer.

The night before Chuckie died, Dad and Mom took some of us to the hospital to be with him. We knew he was not doing well, and thought we might not see him again. When we finally saw Chuckie, we noticed he had retained fluid due to the medications. To us, he now looked like a cherub with his beautiful blue eyes and sweet loving smile.

Oxygen Tent

The little guy was in an oxygen tent. Mom unzipped the tent so we could hold his hand. His big brother remembered, "He seemed to say good-bye to each of us in the most angelic way. We were all crying, but Chuckie was not. He then seemed older than us as if he knew better of what was happening." Most of all, we all remember his eyes. They were still sparkling blue, with his warm sweet smile.

The next day Mom and Dad went into the hospital. Chuckie was much weaker, with little response. Dad always said he did not want to be around when Chuckie died. They were both at his bedside when Dad decided to go downstairs to get some coffee. Mom stayed with Chuckie. Mom unzipped the oxygen tent so she could hold Chuckie's hand, but Chuckie did not respond to her. Instead, he kept looking behind himself, reaching up and back as if someone else was reaching for his hand.

Chuckie died very peacefully while reaching for someone or something that Mom could not see. He took one breath and no more. Chuckie had such a beautiful peaceful expression on his face. A few days later we were at Chuckie's funeral and attended a Mass of the Angels at St. Joseph's Catholic Church. The funeral was very hard for all of us. In the casket Chuckie no longer looked like our Chuckie. He looked more like a Cherub Angel.

What I Remember – What was Most Precious to Me

Remembering Chuckie's:
Big sparkling blue eyes,
Warm, sweet hugs,
Sweet angelic smiles
His sweet hands and feet with the cute space
    between the big toe and second toe
Butterfly kisses,
His can do attitude
Most of all, his unconditional love,
    compassion and empathy
Like an Angel, just passing through, on this earth

Poem for Mom

A few weeks went by. I was a sophomore at school studying literature. I can still remember the Lord Byron poem I was reading, "Prisoner of Chillon." Suddenly, out of nowhere, words were filling my head. I took out a piece of paper and started writing what looked like a poem. It was as if it was Chuckie talking to Mom.

The poem, as I remember, goes like this.

To Mom

Mother, please, try not to weep,
Can't you see I'm just asleep?
Those tears you're shedding are just in vain,
Remember now, I'm no longer in pain.
You may have thought me handicapped,
But, really it was no mishap.
God just sent me for a while,

To try to bring you all a smile.
God meant it to be that way,
To help you recognize and say,
I came to bring you happiness,
Your smiles were more and frowns were less.
Some day you will understand and see,
I am truly where I want to be,
I am in the best place given,
Now, I am with God in Heaven.

Making a difference comes from others too. Chuckie certainly made a difference in my life. Chuckie brought love and happiness into our family. I can still see his angelic smile, as he touched me on my shoulder, reminding me that he was "My Buddy", the angel, just passing through, to watch over us with unconditional love.

Have you ever felt that an angel was watching over you? Sometimes we are fortunate to encounter an angel during our own lifetime, just passing through. When we are blessed to encounter one, we need to tell the story. For me, my angel was my Buddy, Chuckie. ■

ELLEN ARNOTT *BSN, RN, MA*

in Health Education is a former health and wellness executive, business owner and consultant to leading corporations and government agencies.

Ellen began her career as an RN, working in many areas of nursing in the hospital setting before joining AT&T's groundbreaking Disability Assistance Program. The program supported over one million AT&T employees.

After relocating to Texas, Ellen managed Health Services for Abbott Labs and was corporate nursing supervisor for J C Penney's corporate offices until she started and grew her own Nurse Case Management business. Her clients included the Marriott Corporation, Federal Occupational Health, Bureau of Engraving and Printing, Department of Labor, and more.

More recently, Ms. Arnott was a vice president with J.P. Morgan Chase, Health Services. Ellen was responsible for growing the Southwest Region Health Services from two-and-a half nurse-run clinics to 17 nurses supporting 9 clinics in the Southwest U.S. Region.

Ellen was a recipient of the Texas State Achievement Award for Excellence in Occupational Health, and she was a charter member of the Great One-Hundred Nurses in Dallas Texas.

Ellen and her husband live in the Dallas Texas area

CONTACT INFORMATION
Ellen@TheArnotts.com

2

The Orchid Effect: Does Being Different Work For or Against You?

Debjani Biswas

I have always been different—as a female engineer in a predominately male environment; or an Asian leader in the Americas. Sometimes, being different worked for me, sometimes it was a deeply disturbing experience. The question that came to mind was: why do people experience me so differently? Does being different work for, or against, a person?

This phenomenon is called the Orchid Effect—because, it relates to whether being different is seen as being rare and valuable like the flower. And yet, at times, being different is seen as a negative. Why is that?

One of the key factors is bias and prejudice. In 2013, I developed an original framework called the Five Judgments© that relates to the hidden costs of stereotyping. The question is: What are the five critical judgments that are made about a person? Once we understand what these Five Judgments are, we can apply them in multiple areas of our lives.

The Five Judgments©:

These are hidden biases around age, gender, ethnicity, style, education and socioeconomic status, to name a few. Do we label a person as positive or negative based on these judgments? There is a phenomenon in behavioral theory called the 'halo effect'. The halo effect means that you extrapolate one positive or negative experience about a person and apply it to them in everything they do or say. For example, an intern in your organization delivers a high-quality report, on time, for her first project on your team. From that moment on, you assume that everything she does is going to be of high quality and on time. This 'label' follows that individual throughout her career and has significant ramifications on her ultimate success in the workplace.

The Five Judgments are based upon:

- Reputational Currency (buzz)
- Physical Impact (appeal)
- Auditory Cues (sound)
- Distinguishing Markers (differentiators)
- Work Product (output)

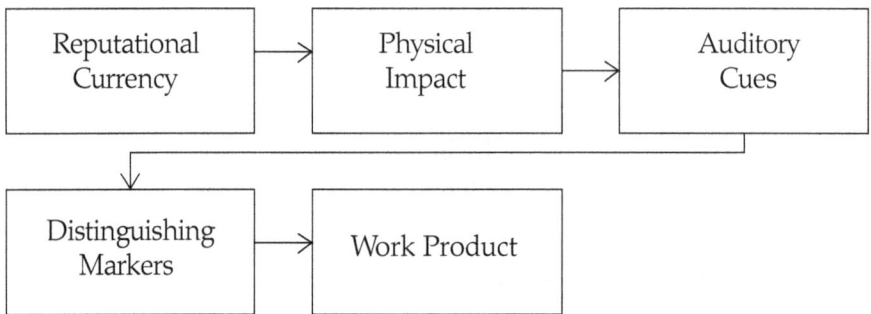

Reputational Currency	→	Physical Impact	→	Auditory Cues

Distinguishing Markers	→	Work Product

Figure 1 Five Judgments Process Flow

The Five Judgments overview:

Reputational Currency: What do people say about you when you are not in a room? What is your 'buzz'? If there is no known data about you, people will make the first judgment based on cultural stereotyping and unconscious biases. This is the reason why Jose Zamora experienced different responses to his applications when he took out a single letter 's' from his name. 'Joe' Zamora received more response, because of the stereotypical assumptions associated with the name Jose (Palmer n.d.). Palmer's specific quote related to the Jose Zamora article: "A 2002 study from researchers at the University of Chicago Graduate School of Business and the Massachusetts Institute of Technology showed that applicants with 'white-sounding names' were 50% more likely to get called for an interview."

Physical Impact: This judgment is not just about whether or not you are attractive or handsome. This has to do with the impression of power or powerlessness that you project, your body language, posture and multiple non verbal messages. We are often overly impressed by what people wear: this includes clothes and accessories. Other factors include hairstyles, age and apparent socioeconomic status. Critical to cultural judgments, your freshness quotient starts with how you smell. More unconscious factors include (in the absence of body odor) the subtle messaging of your fragrance.

Auditory Cues: As a technical woman who coaches and mentors other technical women, there is a definite gender bias in this judgment. Without climbing the slippery slope of generalization, let me share my observations over 20 years of working in multiple industries and across continents. Females tend to speak softer, apologize more, and thus, unfortunately, lose personal power in many interactions. That is not to say that there aren't incredibly assertive, even aggressive women around. Using an engineering mindset of data harvesting and pattern recognition, I am just advising everyone—and females in particular—to be aware of how they sound. Do they sound childish and, in an attempt to be overly appealing, giggle as if they have no gravitas? If the answer is yes, they just lost a lot of power in that moment. How we sound also includes our accent, our choice of words, the timbre of our voice, and how pleasant it appears to be.

Distinguishing Markers: Of all the concepts related to bias and stereotyping, this original phrase that I coined five years ago is the one that has received the strongest positive reinforcement. During my MBA, we learned in Marketing that products have a 'Unique Selling Proposition'—something different that makes them appealing in a 'one of a kind' way. Years later, while reading about DNA, a thought struck me. What if we combined the two disciplines. Do people have, in addition to 'genetic markers', something that makes them unique to the rest of the world? Distinguishing markers may be behavioral, situational or physical—whatever people remember about you after the interaction is over.

Work Product: *What is our output? In a business situation, that is the thing we are paid for.* Sometimes our output is intangible. Those of us who, as parents, put their heart and soul into raising decent, kind, accomplished children do not have tangible 'output' for a very long time. Even at work, it is hard to measure output in some roles. In the absence of real data, output may be measured by proxies such as timeliness or PowerPoint presentation quality. Are you surprised that, often, *four judgments occur before one even starts to examine a person's output?*

These judgments result in an overall "score", which then impacts our success or failure at work. This critical first impression is supplemented over time by perceived future behavior and performance. First impressions are often more important than actual results.

The Orchid Effect©

In some situations, professionally and personally, we feel safe in being authentically different. This, in a nutshell, is the Orchid Effect—where we are perceived as being rare and valuable because of our differences. Unfortunately, all too often we are seen as being the 'squeaky wheel' and are pushed into silence and conformity. Our differences make us 'alien' to others: it isn't so easy to put us in a box, so we may end up being silenced, shunned or patronized.

I called this the Orchid Effect because the Orchid has a brand for being unusual or different. The question is, does being different make people assume that you are rare and valuable like an Orchid? *Or are your differences working against you?*

Awareness and self-management of the Orchid Effect and the Five Judgments can assist anyone in the workplace, even the mainstream population. Regardless of whether you are culturally diverse or not, understanding these dynamics can positively impact your professional and personal brand.

Applications of the framework:

Brand: Reputational Currency

We form opinions about a person's reputation in an instant. It may take as little as fifteen seconds, they say, to form a strong opinion about a person. In fact, you don't even have to meet someone to have a strong opinion about them… and I am not just talking about celebrities!

If there is sufficient buzz or word of mouth about a person, that information quickly morphs into a reputation. If there is no information about the person, then cultural stereotyping causes the interviewer (in our example) to fill in the blanks based upon assumptions about the group the interviewee represents.

Personal Appeal: Physical Impact, Auditory Cues, and Distinguishing Markers

Next comes the moment of actual contact. Things like appearance, dress, and sound weigh in—in that order—often occurring simultaneously. If there is something culturally distinguishing about the person, that data is unconsciously filed away as well. Some of these data points are a good indicator of workplace success and some of them are not.

Work Product: Tangible Output

By the time the hiring manager (in an interview situation) reaches the output or work product stage, four judgments have already been made. Two key takeaways: the candidate may never get a chance to show work product, due to the negative impact of the first four judgments; second, neither party (interviewer or candidate, in this example) may be aware of the strong, unconscious dynamics underpinning the surface interaction.

All Five Judgments culminate in the Orchid Effect. This is the categorization of an individual as being an Orchid because they are unique and differentiated, as opposed to being rejected for the task or position because of diversity.

Cost of Stereotyping in the Workplace: The Orchid Effect is important because there is a very real cost associated with not valuing differences.

Scenario: Interview of candidates A and B for a program manager position for a large, cross-functional international project.

Candidate A: The buzz around this person is good—one of his friends is your marketing contact and recommended him. He is personable, well dressed, and well spoken, and exudes confidence and poise. He arrives on time for his interview and is knowledgeable about the thrilling five-set tennis match at the Australian Open, or the incredible ending to the latest Super Bowl (depending on the country in which this interview is taking place). He promises to send you an example of his last big program and the software tools he used after the interview is over.

Candidate B is an unknown quantity. She applied online through the company recruiting process. She is dressed neatly but not particularly smartly. Her English is good but her name is hard to pronounce. She has no perfume and you detect a mild, sweaty odor as she comes closer. Her palms are clammy when you shake hands. You make a comment about the sporting event referenced earlier and she looks blankly at you. As you smile and exchange pleasantries you speculate that she has low social skills and is a little different. She pulls out a folder with some glowing references and a sample project plan, using new tracking software that you have not seen before. You note down the name of that software so you can give it to Candidate A later.

What just happened?

Somewhere between the third and fourth judgments, you made a selection decision that Candidate A would be a better program manager than Candidate B. What happened is known as the Orchid Effect. *Based on mostly subjective decision-making processes, you also decided that Candidate A is a better organizational fit for the job.* The Orchid Effect was negative for Candidate B. Based on cues such as lower physical appeal and lack of knowledge of current sporting events, you categorized her on the negative end of the spectrum: different enough to be rejected for the position.

When you selected Candidate A over Candidate B, did you make the right decision?

Possibly. However, there is a good *chance that you made an incorrect, highly costly hiring decision based on factors not pertaining to the job at hand.*

Let's analyze both the candidates using spider web charts depicting relative strengths and weaknesses for the position of program manager. This is a visual summary of the cost of stereotyping that is a result of the Five Judgments.

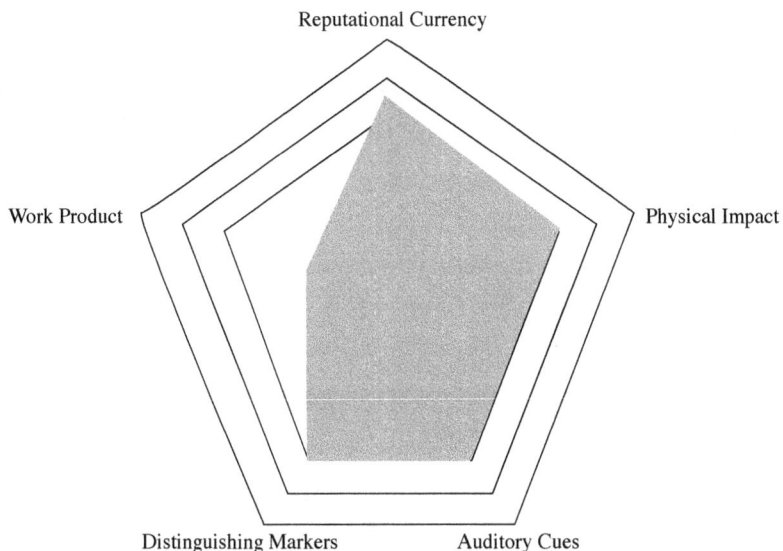

Figure 2 Cost of Stereotyping: Candidate A Selected

Candidate A is selected for a program manager role due to a positive read on the first four judgments, though his work product, output, and overall dollar value to the organization may be lower than those of Candidate B.

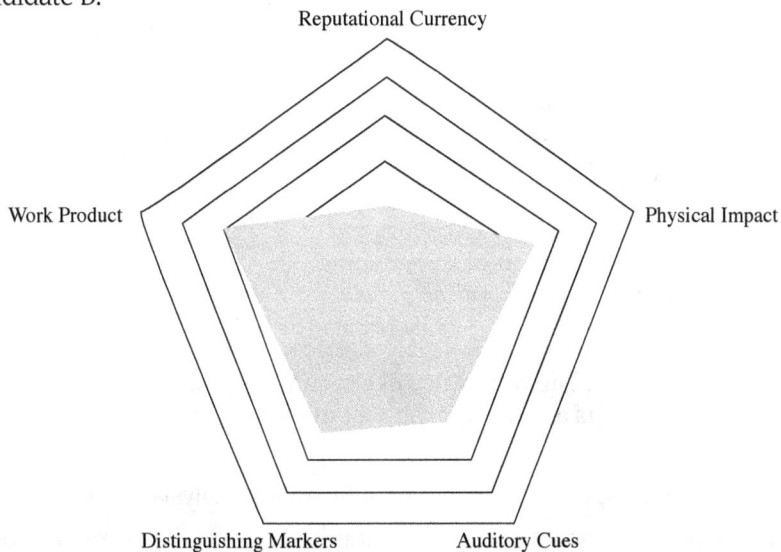

Figure 3 Cost of Stereotyping: Candidate B Rejected

Candidate B is rejected due to the first four judgments, though her work output may be higher. The Orchid Effect, as a result of the Five Judgments, is that Candidate B is "too different" and will not be a good fit for the organization. I take this as a proxy for the cost of stereotyping, of not using the Orchid Effect in our interactions.

Let us now overlay the two diagrams. I have also added numbers for each of the judgments, on a scale of 1 to 10, where higher means it is a more positive judgment.

This will give us a comparative visual, which relates to the very real cost of stereotyping in the workplace.

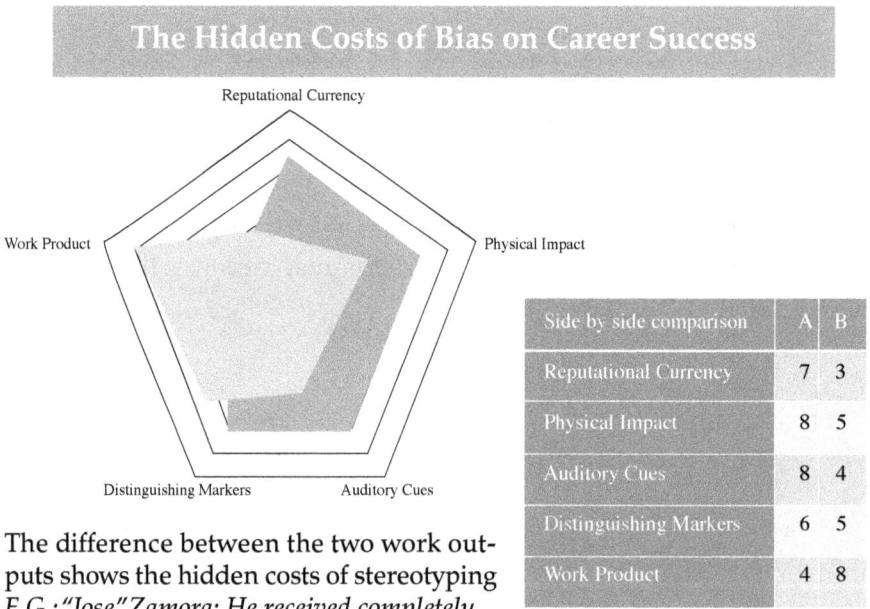

The Hidden Costs of Bias on Career Success

Reputational Currency

Work Product

Physical Impact

Distinguishing Markers   Auditory Cues

Side by side comparison	A	B
Reputational Currency	7	3
Physical Impact	8	5
Auditory Cues	8	4
Distinguishing Markers	6	5
Work Product	4	8

The difference between the two work outputs shows the hidden costs of stereotyping E.G.: "Jose" Zamora: He received completely different resume response rates just by removing one letter from his name!

Figure 4: The difference between work products (8-4) is a proxy for the cost of stereotyping.

Author's note: Obviously this is a multivariate analysis. Cultural stereotyping is not the only dynamic occurring here. Ageism or sexism (limiting beliefs about the abilities of females in technical areas, for example) may kick in as well. There is the possibility of cultural stereotyping in each of the judgments. For example, how ethnic a person looks is a 'physical impact' judgment, as a foreign accent is one based on 'auditory cues'.

Managing the Orchid Effect successfully as an interviewer:

Now that we understand the Five Judgments, let's say we are interviewing a culturally diverse candidate for the same program manager role. What are some things we can do to manage our Orchid Effect or tendency to reject people who are perceived as being negatively different from us?

- The first step is always self awareness. We are all human, and therefore have deeply held beliefs, which translate to behavioral preferences. Sometimes, these manifest as biases.
- Focus on the requirements for the role, the assignment, the task at hand. If we make a hiring decision based on those requirements, before we interact with the person, our choices are more unbiased. *It is no coincidence that on the TV show 'The Voice' blind auditions unearth incredible vocal talent, sometimes packaged in unconventional physical characteristics.*
- If possible, try to shake or displace the limiting beliefs that no longer apply. Changing limiting beliefs is difficult but possible over time with determination and will.

Once you become aware of cultural and other stereotypes from your self-assessment on limiting beliefs, focus on the requirements for the role:

Reverse the order of the judgments. If it's for a program manager role, analyze the job requirements. What needs to be achieved, by when, for this position? Make sure you cover those questions first. Get examples of work product. Use references to ask previous employees about output. Minimize the effect of superficial judgments. This applies to non-cultural stereotypes as well. If we make the most of our hiring decision based on tangible job requirements, will we not, over time, get a closer match for the role? As you read this sentence, some of you are indignantly remarking: There is nothing new in this; that's what I always do.

No, you don't.

Trust me on this one. If you are human, you don't.

If possible, try to shake or displace the limiting beliefs that no longer apply: This is the most difficult but typically the most rewarding aspect of taking a diversity foray. Feedback lies all around us, if we are only willing to receive it and then act on it. Sometimes we change our actions and then our beliefs follow suit. My advice: take baby steps to change your limiting behaviors first. A simple action is taking the time to learn how diverse people pronounce their names. Many of them came from another country with nothing but a suitcase and their name. It is a sign of respect to try and learn how to pronounce their names. And if it's a long and difficult one, then ask for their permission to fail while you learn it. They will appreciate the effort.

To summarize: Be aware of your biases, and how superficial judgments may be clouding the accuracy of the Orchid Effect. Focus on what is required for the job, the role, and the project and give work content more importance than subjective opinions and feelings in the decision.

Let us focus first, second, and always on the product or work at hand. Can we become more self-aware and be willing to acknowledge that we have unconscious biases? If so, we are ready to take a "Diversity Foray" together. I coined this phrase because each of the *Dos* starts with the letter 'A'—and there are four of them. So, transforming 'four-a' into 'foray'—which means journey or exploration, we can improve our multicultural and multistyle savvy. Why do I now bring style into the picture? That is because we also make judgments based on whether people are introverted or extraverted, assertive or more unassuming.

There are *dos* and *don'ts* in this Diversity Foray.

A Diversity Foray© - Global Toolkit for Multicultural Competence* (Biswas 2013)

Do	Don't
Ask	Shun
Accept	Patronize
Adapt	Assume
Appreciate	Crumble
	Escalate

*A detailed explanation of the Diversity Foray is available in *Unleash the Power of Diversity*, Mukherjee Biswas 2013, AH Publications.

If we follow this simple toolkit and combine it with Emotional Intelligence, we will practice the Orchid Effect with positive impact and results. This, then is the future for us—learning, helping, teaching each other with 'graceful, flawed authenticity.'

As the late great Maya Angelou said:

"People will forget what you said, people will forget what you did, but people will never forget how you made them feel."

Make sure you make them feel as rare and valuable as an orchid. They, and you, may never be the same again!

DEBJANI BISWAS.

Vision: Learning, helping, teaching with graceful flawed authenticity.

Power Leader Debjani Biswas *has a unique blend of executive and corporate experience (PepsiCo, Texas Instruments) and education (Chemical Engineering, MBA, Executive Coaching). An NAPW 'Woman of the Year' recipient, she serves on the Board of Directors of her Engineering Alumni Organization IITNT.*

Change Agent: *As a Fortune 50 executive, Biswas experienced the global epidemic of the 'miserably successful'. Facing adversity, she made a transformational career shift. President of Coachieve, LLC., Biswas is currently a keynote speaker (Ericcson, Takeda, UNH, Kennecott.) author, trusted strategist for CEOs. After her book was selected in Barnes & Noble stores, she completed a U.S. Barnes & Noble Book Tour. Her groundbreaking frameworks are being used in 23 countries.*

Key Platform: *The business and personal impact of inclusion and diversity. Biswas applies emotional intelligence and an engineering mindset of data harvesting—pattern recognition to complex business situations.*

- Unleash the Power of Diversity *2013 Multi-Cultural Competence http://amzn.to/160FcZz*
- Miserably Successful No More *2017 Multi-Style Competence & Stress Reduction.*
- *Endorsed by Marshall Goldsmith - Thinkers50 Award Winner for Most Influential Leader Thinker in the World; bestselling author of* Mojo *and* Triggers:

For keynotes, please email contact@coachieve.us

3

Living with Courage and Trust
Joan Chalkley

From when I was nine years of age, I always loved springboard diving. It's a fun sport with some very interesting characters. I mean, who in her right mind flings herself off of a diving board to flip and spin and risk landing flat on the water? Divers. Because they are a bit crazy, they can be really fun people! In the sport of diving—as in many sports and in life—one's success depends on courage.

In diving, whenever it is time to learn a new dive, it takes courage to get up there and try it for the first time. It also requires trust in your coach. After all, s/he is the one who decides when you are ready for the new dive. Imagine learning a back dive from the high board. It requires falling backwards through the air without seeing where you are going and blindly landing head first in the water. To this day, I remember my first try. I landed flat on my stomach from my head to my toes. Perhaps I was turning black and blue even before I could crawl out of the water! Let's not call this a failure. Heck, I learned something from it—go slower as you fall back to start the dive. Learning this, I practiced more from the low board, and when my coach felt I was ready, it took courage to get up to the high board and try it again. My second try was successful—I landed headfirst! Today, I still love diving, and the back dive is my favorite dive on the three-meter board.

In diving, it's not just the times when you learn a new dive that require courage and trust. It is really every practice, even in the small things. For example, if your coach tells you that you are too close to the board and you need to move the dive back, will you make the proper correction or will you avoid practicing the dive? If you want to continue to be a diver, you'll need to do that dive again. My theory is to reduce fear as much as possible. By doing the dive immediately following, that fearful state doesn't stay with you very long. Your mind can go back on the "I can do this dive" track, by taking charge of the thoughts running through your mind.

There are many simple decisions in life that require the same kind of courage and trust as diving. For example, if you need to ask for help with something—perhaps an assignment at work—do you ask another person in the office if you are stuck or don't know how to proceed? Perhaps you think to yourself, "I don't want to bother them" or "They will think that I'm dumb if I ask." It takes courage to ask. Take control of your thoughts. What is your main objective in completing this assignment? Hopefully, it is to do the best job possible for your company. Choosing to be vulnerable by asking the question and working together with your team will make you more valuable and give you an opportunity to grow, even in small ways.

Let's look at bigger ways—when life throws you a curve ball. I was diagnosed with breast cancer. After my regular mammogram, my doctor recommended additional tests and a biopsy. I was in my office at work when I received a phone call telling me that I had Stage Two cancer in my right breast. That "C" word produces fear in any of us. I asked myself, "How can I approach this life event with courage and trust?" This meant finding out all I could about what would be coming with the surgery. It meant making sure that I had a good doctor who I could trust and that I evaluated alternatives. This life event was not a choice for me, yet I could choose how I felt and thought and acted. I did not want to panic. I did not want to share my condition with many people as they could have become fearful, projecting that onto me. We had a family vacation planned to Italy. I decided to go and enjoy the trip and set up the necessary appointments for when we returned. After surgery, radiation was recommended and could cause exhaustion. With this situation which seemed out of control, I wanted to control something. So, I targeted completion of my radiation treatments by Memorial Day weekend. I set up regular appointments at 3:00 pm. This was something that I could control. Then, after the appointment on treatment days, I would go do something I loved. For me, it was walking my dog or watching my daughter at her middle school softball practice. In so doing, I could focus on the joy in each of these days, and not let my mind wander to the potential fear of the situation.

Sometimes, our decisions may not be triggered by life events. Sometimes, they may be self-initiated. For me, it was a decision about where I lived. I had been living in Dallas, Texas, for almost thirty years. Then one day, I heard a speaker talking about "Changing Lanes," and I asked myself if this is where I wanted to live ten years from now. And if not in Dallas, where would I want to be? I decided that it would be South Florida. This was a logical, thought-out decision since my brother and two girlfriends lived in the same area. Yet, it was a bit impulsive since I had lived in Dallas for so long. A move like this isn't simple. It would take work. It would take planning. There were some important things to work out: Could I find a job? Where would I live?

I headed off to Boca Raton without a job, trusting I would be able to find one, and being there would make it easier. My friend, Margaret, and her husband offered to share their home with me for as long as I needed. With a few plans in place and a lot of trust, off I went to Boca Raton, Florida, over Independence Day weekend. I have been blessed by how well this move has turned out. Yes, I had to do my part. I had applied for jobs online before leaving Texas and was offered a position by the third week of July. The position was in IT software development as a project manager, working with wonderful people in a great corporate culture. I relied on Margaret and Pete who shared their home with me for four months. Then, I was blessed to find a wonderful townhouse in Boca

Raton, and, as my friend Lisa would say, "We are living the dream!"

I believe that we can all be "living the dream" by having the courage to trust in one another. The dream is found in our heart—not in what we have, whom we know, or what we've done. Each of us has been created in His image, and each of us has talents and knowledge to share. It will take courage to overcome self-doubt in many of life's situations. In each of those moments, appreciate how truly blessed you are to face the decision. Realize that you'll learn and grow from a decision made, even if it doesn't come out as you had hoped.

In order to live life to the fullest, to be "living the dream," go out with courage to make choices, trust that you are on the right path, and be grateful for so many of the wonderful things in your life.

JOAN CHALKLEY *has her Master's Degree in Human Relations and Business. She has been an information technology project manager for over thirty years. Professionally, Joan is a certified PMP (Project Management Professional). Her life-long passion for the sport of springboard diving is demonstrated by her participation in masters' diving national and international competitions. Joan holds over fifty national titles and one international title, and she has received All-American honors. Giving back to her sport, Joan has coached some talented divers—one receiving a full-ride scholarship to The Ohio State University. Additionally, Joan has served on the USA Diving Board of Directors, has been the USA Masters National Chairperson, and has supported USA Diving through her volunteer efforts as national meet director, registration chairperson, and as a FINA Internationally certified judge. Her philosophy on life is to live joyfully and abundantly while being a blessing to those around her. Be an atmosphere creator!*

CONTACT INFORMATION
joan.chalkley@att.net

4

Gone But Not Forgotten
Going through pain has no gain;
Growing through pain has great gain

Mary Hershberger

It was just another day on our small farm, nestled in Southeastern Ohio. It was the fall of 2006, and like the rest of the families in our Amish community, we were working hard to support our growing family.

In 1993 when I was 14 years old, I met William, the new young man who had started working in the community. He was six-and-a-half years older than me, so I didn't "officially" meet him until three years later when I joined the youth group. We got to know each other very well and were good friends, but I never thought of him as a future husband! Unknown to me, he'd had his eyes on me before I joined the youth group, so when he first asked me out on a date, I turned him down! (This is my children's favorite part about us getting to know each other!) But his charm soon won me over, and we started dating in June of 1998.

On October 21, 1999, four days after my 20th birthday, William and I got married. Young and in love, and just having married the man of my dreams…what could go wrong, right? Well, living in an imperfect world like we do, life has many challenges along the way. And William and I were not exempt from those challenges!

In the year 2000, we were so excited to become first-time parents to a beautiful baby girl! Now we were a family of three, and our lives had changed forever. Eight months before her arrival, we had bought thirty acres of land with no buildings so my husband had built us a small house and buggy shed (garage), and he was now working on building a barn. We had the barn raising on our first wedding anniversary! Now that the buildings were up, he was ready to start his business. He owned and operated a furniture shop, Sandy Ridge Hardwoods.

A year later we welcomed our second baby girl—our family was growing fast! By 2006, we were the parents of five little children! And life had not dealt us the easiest hand. We had lots of sickness in our home. Our oldest daughter had leukemia when she was three. Our oldest son, the third child, was born with heart problems. When I was pregnant with our fourth child, I was bedridden with blood clots in my legs and anemia. Our fourth child, the second son, was born a healthy baby but soon afterwards developed a severe rash that was the equivalent of second-degree burns covering his whole body. So here we were, a young family with five children and three of them were sick.

We discovered that the materials we used to build the house, in combination with mold, were poisoning our family. So we did some renovations to our house, and everyone seemed to be recovering well.

Things had been going very well until one afternoon in early December. William offered to pick up our daughter from school that afternoon since he had a young horse that needed the exercise. On his way to school, the horse spooked because of a metal rod along the side of the road and tipped the open buggy, throwing him out. The steel wheels went over his neck crushing his atlas, the top vertebrae. He got up, ran after the horse and caught him! When he came home he was covered in blood and had a throbbing headache, but he refused to see a doctor and asked me to clean him up.

At the time of the accident, we were unaware of the extent of the injury to his neck. He knew he was in a lot of pain, but he figured it was just some bumps and bruises and would be healed up within a week or so. Had we known, however, we would have taken different actions. By the time the doctors found the problem years later, it was too late to do surgery and the damage was permanent. It was a hard truth to accept. The doctor who finally found it explained to us that the atlas is the only vertebrae that you can break and still be able to get around.

At this time in our life's journey, we were not Christians. We were Amish and taught that following the rules and regulations of the Amish law was not to be questioned. To break a rule of that law required a public confession in church, and if it was a major rule being disobeyed, it was a public confession and a public punishment in church.

The Amish would profess to be Christians, but they didn't believe in being born again. They believe that when you say you are saved, you have been led astray by reading too much. They taught mostly about the authority/fear of God, but they never taught that He was a loving, kind God to be in a relationship with. The Amish ordnance is their most revered and feared authority. In fact, when we were being *interrogated* just before we left the Amish, the Bishop said that he had come to the conclusion that we had decided to hold the Bible higher than the Amish ordnance! And we were thinking, *we sure hope so!* We had also been taught that if we ever left the Amish we would go straight to hell because that was the greatest sin a person could commit. So having that fear in your heart meant you didn't even entertain the thought of doing it…or so I thought!

The Bible says that we are created in God's image and in His likeness (Genesis 1:27) and that the Word shall be preached in all the world in every nation (Matthew 24:14). And since we are created in His image, we are created to love and be loved, and to be in a relationship with Him. That is man's natural habitat. Water is a fish's natural habitat. Just as a fish can't survive out of water, so you can't survive without being in a relationship with God. So when the word was preached to us, we were like the fish that was stuck on the shore until someone came along and threw him in the water! We were now swimming in the sea of love—a love we had never known before! The blinders were taken from our eyes, and we could see the truth for the first time.

Now that the truth was revealed to us, we had a decision to make. Would we allow the fear of man to stop us from following Jesus, or would we trust God with our future? It was a hard decision and one that only someone who has gone through will understand, but we made a life-altering decision that would change our lives and our children's lives for generations to come. We decided to leave the Amish! It was with a mixture of joy and sorrow. Joy in our new-found faith no doubt, but sad knowing that we would be shunned by the church and would never be able to interact with our friends and family who we were leaving behind.

The freedom we were experiencing in our new-found faith in Jesus was amazing. Nonetheless, we were brought back to reality with my husband's condition. After several weeks, the cuts and bruises on the outside were healed, but the headaches continued. This was now early spring of 2007. He started noticing some numbness in his legs, but he still didn't see the need for a doctor. He had spent a lot of money on his family over the past several years with all the health issues we were having and no health insurance. He wasn't about to do the same on himself!

His debilitation rapidly progressed to the point he couldn't walk anymore. One morning he woke up, and his kidneys and bowels had shut down—you might say his whole body had shut down. I took him to the hospital, and the doctors quickly did some tests thinking he had cancer or some kind of debilitating disease like multiple sclerosis or Lou Gehrig's disease. All the tests came back negative. I had tried telling the doctors the man had an accident. He was not sick—he was hurt! But since it had been several months since the accident, they didn't think that it could be related. After several weeks in the hospital and the tests still coming back negative, they decided that with the symptoms he was having, they would call it MS and send us home with that diagnosis.

By this time, I was pregnant with our youngest son. William kept losing mobility and was in a wheelchair full time. It was a trying time for all of us. The children were losing their daddy, who they thought was the greatest man they had ever known. I was losing my husband, who had been my constant companion through the good times and the hard times. He was one of the most caring people I have ever known. He was not perfect, but to this day, my children believe he was!

When we face trials like these, we have incredible choices to make. We can choose to blame God and become bitter, or we can trust Him in the midst of it all and become better. Remembering that God is not the author of sickness is important. The Bible says that the enemy came to steal, kill, and destroy, but Jesus came to give us life and life more abundantly (John 10:10). When you are in a seemingly hopeless situation it can be very challenging to choose to encourage yourself.

> *Remember my friends, we have not a high priest who cannot be touched with the feelings of our infirmities but was in all points tempted like as we are, yet without sin. Let us therefore come boldly unto the throne of grace that we may obtain mercy, and find grace to help in time of need.*
> (Hebrews 4:15 and 16).

He knows what you are feeling, so come to Him boldly. Don't run away from Him when you most need Him, denying His grace in a time you most desperately need Him.

I wish I could say I always make the right decisions, but unfortunately that is not the case. I did learn, however, that when I choose to trust God, no matter how dramatic a situation I am in, he is faithful. Proverbs 30:5 says that "Every word of God is pure, and he is a shield on to them that put their trust in him." This was one of my favorite verses, and still is. I like to remind myself that it is God's responsibility to shield me from things too overwhelming for me, but my job is to trust him in every situation. He has been very faithful to me!

In March of 2008, William came down with pneumonia and ended up being in the hospital for three weeks. Also in that same month, our youngest son, William, Jr. was born. My husband had been moved to the nursing home on the 25th of March, and on the 26th, William Jr.

was born. William was in the nursing home for six months, and then we moved him home. Finally our family was back together! By this time, William had debilitated to where he spent most of his time in a hospital bed in our living room.

For the next several years, he continued to lose strength. He lost his speech and ability to swallow food or water. So we had to put in a feeding tube. I couldn't handle the thought of my husband being on formula, so I got together a recipe that I felt would provide him with the necessary nutrition for an adult, and we would blend it into a puree so it was thin enough to go through the feeding tube. Our two oldest daughters did an incredible job in helping out, anything from washing the dishes, to entertaining the little ones, to giving their daddy his food through the tube. William also had to have a trachea put in so he wouldn't choke on his own saliva.

I can only imagine how things looked from William's perspective. I cannot imagine how humbling it must have been for him to have his own daughters feed him, and to lay there day after day not being able to talk, with those days turning into weeks, and weeks into months, and months into years. He spent most of his time listening to messages, speakers, books, and the Bible on CD. The children loved to see the smile on his face as they brought him a handful of wildflowers, or a card they made for him, or a simple note saying "# 1 Daddy!" The older ones would sit on his bed and read stories to him while little William Jr. just loved crawling all over him and pulling tubes he shouldn't!

Throughout the six years of his illness, he was in and out of the hospital a lot, and he would have to stay longer and longer as his body continued to debilitate. In 2010, we ended up having to put him on a ventilator. He just didn't have enough strength to breathe on his own. Our way of communicating was I would try to be very specific with my questions so he could respond with a yes or no by nodding his head. But the time came when he couldn't move his head, so I would watch his eyes. He would turn them one way for yes and another for no. I am so thankful that we were able to communicate.

The day of his departure came. It was in March of 2012. In the beginning of March, the doctors believed he had an aneurysm in his brain stem which left him in a coma-like state for the last three weeks of his life. After the complete round of tests, I had to make a decision that no one wants to make for a loved one. They told me that he was completely dependent on life support and was not responding at all. So I had a meeting with some family members, and we decided that the time had come for us to let them pull the tubes. He entered the Gates of Heaven on March 31, 2012.

Death is so final. I knew the time had come and thought I was ready to face it. But when that last breath is taken, that thread of hope that you were clinging to is gone. The hope that the children would someday have their daddy back. The hope of walking hand-in-hand with the man I loved. The dreams of a family vacation at the beach, or the pride he would have taken in taking his daughters out on their first date. I would have well-meaning people say to me things like "Well, at least you were prepared since he was sick for so long."

Let me tell you something, you cannot prepare for the death of a loved one. Even though I thought I was prepared, I was not. There's just no easy way to lose a loved one. I tend to think it would be easier to have it happen unexpectedly because you would be living a full, good quality life, and you wouldn't have death staring you in the face year after year.

Independent from how we lose them, God is so gracious and desires for us to let Him carry us through. When we choose to lean on Him in our most difficult situations, we will experience our greatest victories. Choosing to praise Him in every situation, not *for* every situation, but *in* every situation. Praising God for who He is. Because sometimes we find ourselves in a situation that we created for ourselves, and it's not a good one. So we don't thank God for that, but we praise Him for His goodness to us as we walk through whatever we find ourselves in. He is a gentleman. He will not force himself on you, but He is right there when we invite him in!

Yay though I walk through the valley of the shadow of death, I will fear no evil, for thou art with me. Thy rod and thy staff they comfort me.

(Psalms 23:4)

Without His presence and grace in the children's and my life, I have no idea where we would be. But we are not without Him! I have seen my children triumphantly walking through this, and I couldn't be more proud of them. We love talking about Daddy and reminiscing about his life. Talking about him to the children keeps him alive in their lives. They love when I say, "That is something Daddy would have done." I believe that is very important to a child who has lost their daddy. They have just experienced a huge loss, and if you don't talk about their daddy, they will not only have lost their daddy, but will also lose the legacy. That need not happen.

I have been blessed with a great man for a husband and father to our children. It was just too short a journey! His legacy will be with us for generations to come!

A father to the fatherless and protector of widows is God in his holy habitation.

Psalm 68:5 ESV

The mountains shall depart, and the hills be removed; but my kindness shall not depart from thee, neither shall the Covenant of my peace be removed says the Lord that has Mercy on thee.

Isaiah 54:10 KJV

God has been an amazing Father to my children and a loving husband/protector to me! Though we miss William as a father and husband every day, we have chosen to walk forward triumphantly and not allow tragedy to mold us, but rather the Word of God! ■

MARY HERSHBERGER *lives on a small farm in Southeastern Ohio with her six children. She is a stay-at-home mother, homeschooling her children. She is also the owner of a small business, Sapphire Properties of Ohio. She is a firm believer that God blesses those who position and prepare themselves for His blessings. (Deuteronomy 28)*

CONTACT INFORMATION
Mary Hershberger
hershfamof7@gmail.com

5

Enthusiasm:
Are You Living a Loving or Fearful Life?

Ljilja Hubbard

I'm here to ask you this...what kind of life do you want? What kind of life do you have and live now? The better question is...what kind of society do we want to live in? If we were all happy with our lives and things were perfect in society, this book would end here with the first paragraph.

Good...you didn't put the book down! That means you do want a better life that will in turn bring change into our society and create a better place to live. Our world has so many sad and devastating things happening today. Change is needed now...not tomorrow or someday. Let's give ourselves a present in the now and create a world we are happy and joyful to live in. It's my hope to start a movement that will bring joy and love back into the world—in the form of enthusiasm.

The best way to cheer yourself up is to try to cheer somebody else up.
~Mark Twain

My search started when I decided it was time for me to share my story and shine my light into the world, allowing others to feel that they, too, can do it. That thought process comes from my favorite poem by Marianne Williamson, *"A Return to Love."*

My journey to explore enthusiasm and how it shows up in the world started back in August 2016. I went to a personal growth class, Heart of a Warrior, where I was on a support team for a group of incredible individuals, now Warriors. I met a friend there, Ninja Warrior, who reminded me very much of a younger version of myself and exemplified the enthusiasm I was going to write about. The class was two-and-a-half days long, and it showed me that coming from a place of love and joy is a choice we all get to make—allowing our vulnerability to come out rather than putting up walls during our difficult times. When we open up, an inner freedom is created making one more mindful and aware—that experience allows room for more enthusiasm and joy.

It's as easy as making the decision to want to be better and figuring out *WHY* it's important to make a difference. Then with that decision, desire and understanding, it becomes a choice…what do you choose daily? To smile or be grumpy? How do you start your day? Ready to give it 100% and be all in, or do you have hesitation because you are not happy with something going on?

After the class, I needed a ride to the airport to get home to my boys. Ninja Warrior graciously offered to take me. That ride was the beginning of some amazing things in my life and the start of a great friendship. I realized that my dream to write was tucked way deep inside my heart where NO ONE could touch it or make fun of it. My new friend somehow got me to talk about a dream that I hadn't told anyone for the past five years. It's been tucked away just waiting in the dark for the right time.

Well, the time was now! Or was it? I didn't know the first thing about writing. *STOP!!! DON'T SAY ANOTHER WORD! People will NOT accept you. They will MAKE FUN OF YOU…You won't ever finish the book and it will be yet another thing in your life you FAIL at!*

WOW, I had to take a deep breath at that point. This feeling—deep down—was F-E-A-R. This negative cloud of pessimism, skepticism, bad, rejecting and weak emotions that want to get us down and keep us from achieving what we want. The fear was bubbling up from my stomach. It was taunting me to say, "I was JUST kidding about the book and being a published author."

Ninja Warrior was already a published author, so I was a little intimidated by her. Even though I was daunted, I committed to going with her to beautiful Captiva Island, Florida. It was amazing. The four days spent there were life changing. The belief my fear created was a false sense of security. My disillusion made me migrate towards the comfort I felt in my fear—it was my place of protection from failure, pain, and betrayal. When we come from a place of love, we learn to trust ourselves, and that's when everything changes. The natural outcome is optimism, calmness, strength, belief, and positivity. I was "stuck in the muck" as they say, and knew if I could push through it and shine my light, I would be an example for others that anything is possible.

I was so excited (and nervous) to share my experience and the valuable lessons I learned about fear with my boys. However, that old friend nervousness had taken residency at the front door. Running away only pushes us deeper into the darkness and despair of the moment. We can all relate to who was waiting...*How dare you come home happy? You know it's time to come back to reality.* When our fear creates urgency, we run. Where do we go? Why do we go there? Typically, we run to safety. I was reacting to my fear rather than being motivated by love. Fear waits for us all in an attempt to steal our joy and hold us hostage, keeping us from being our authentic loving selves.

I was over the moon to see my boys when they came home from school. I started writing after I got settled. My older son, seventeen, came home, and we talked a bit and then my younger son, fourteen, arrived. It was a pretty normal start to the evening until the tension between my boys began. The tension turned to arguing. Mom got involved, and they were both sent to their rooms. I was deflated and felt beaten up. All that excitement, energy and love. It went out the door, and my fear just let loose again. Why is that? How did it change so quickly? Have you ever experienced that deflation or emptiness?

Talking with my younger son in his room, the conversation just turned ugly. There was no way to turn it around, and I was just making it worse with every single breath I took—I was devastated. My son decided he had enough with the tension he and his brother shared. He decided to leave his home in Wisconsin to go live with his dad in California. My worst nightmare had come to life. All I could think was *How did I fail? How did I allow this toxin in my house? How did I allow things to escalate and get this bad?* It was all about me because I was not able to think clearly. I was consumed with the fear of losing a piece of my heart and soul. That was all I could focus on.

Did I *beg* him to stay? Did I *apologize* for getting angry? Did I do the *most important thing* a mom can do? NOOOOO!!! I was paralyzed. I was not thinking about the pain, hurt, confusion, or feeling of betrayal my fourteen-year-old son was dealing with. All I could do was think of myself. I said, "If that's going to make you happy, call your father right now." As soon as those words hit my lips, I wanted to take them back.

My son said, "No, I'll call him tomorrow, Mom."

"Why wait?" *S-T-U-P-I-D, what are you doing?* REALLY?? Did I just do that? My inner voice was screaming at me.

"Well, I won't go until the end of the school year," he responded.

Not very composed at this point, I blurted out, "Why wait? If you don't like it here and it's better for you away from us at your Dad's, no reason to wait until the end of the year!"

NO REASON TO WAIT? Holy Cow! Did I REALLY just say that??? *Just STOP and give him a hug, say you understand and let's not make any decisions right now.* I was digging a hole that was getting deeper and baited him to keep going. Have you ever felt hijacked like that? It was like an out of body experience. I was watching myself—my fearful thoughts rendered me helpless, and I was paralyzed from doing anything different.

"Call your Dad, and if you still want to go after you talk to him, I will be sad and won't stop you." Sadly, that's where the conversation ended.

I love my son so much that in an effort to keep him with me, my fear got in the way, and my nervousness took over and actually created what I feared most.

"If you think you can do a thing or think you can't do a thing, you're right."

~ Henry Ford

I realized with that situation that love and fear are two things we battle every day of our lives. If we allow all the bad things in life to create negativity and a toxic atmosphere around us, how will we ever succeed? If we create a positive and loving atmosphere, imagine how that would change our world and then bleed into society. I really love Henry Ford's positivity. He said, "Coming together is a beginning, staying together is progress, and working together is success." It's my hope that each of us go out into the world after reading this and make a choice to come together in love, stay together to change the world we live in, and work together so we can have a more peaceful life where everyone helps each other.

Showing up daily with enthusiasm is as easy as choosing to see the good and looking at things that happen in life through the eyes of love, versus fear. You're probably thinking, "Yeah, that is a lot easier said than done, Lady!" Well, YES, you are correct. The difficulty is we are all consumed by our own daily living and situations. This is normal. However, what if we saw each other as brothers and sisters instead of a handicapped person, neighbor, co-worker, boss, or stranger? Why must everything have a label? We are all equal—a family of the world—and when we send our love out unconditionally instead of putting labels on it or expectations, people feel they matter and respond in kindness rather than in fear. Fearful responses like: *What do they want from me? Why are they being nice to me? They can't really be that nice!*

If I give something to someone and expect something back from them, I am only creating more entitlement thinking in the world. Most people find it difficult to come from a place of love rather than fear. A place of true, unconditional, agape love (like in the Bible) that has no expectation of receiving—only an overabundance of giving.

Have you ever wondered what life would be like if fear never crossed your mind or heart? Or if all the prejudice, anger, skepticism, and destruction in our world just faded away? Why do we as a society find it easier to hold on to all the toxic negativity that we see every day—on social media, the news, at work, at home—and carry that with us everywhere we go?

People, life is too short not to carry joy in your heart and have enthusiasm for life. I see people every day who are on autopilot and just go through the motions of life. Life is meant to be enjoyed. We all have a purpose on this Earth. The trick is to find our WHY and learn to share our gifts in a way that honors life and enthusiasm rather than tearing its beauty apart with fear and hatred.

There are seasons in life. Some of us never see a cold and dark season. Some of us never see the sun and warmth of life. In what season is your life? Where is your heart? What mindset do you allow yourself to carry with you every day? I've lived many seasons in my life—personally and professionally.

What does that mean you ask? I've experienced the sun of summer when I first got married and had children. I've made my way through the wet of spring when my marriage started to fail. The chill of fall was pretty scary when I realized I was going to be a single mom with two amazing boys. I've even survived the cold of winter. Reality hit as a single mom when I found myself divorced, and had lost my job and my mother in the same twelve-month period of time. I've lived and experienced much happiness and joy, which shined like the summer. I've also experienced much hurt, sadness, and betrayal in life—the despair and cold of winter.

Regardless of what I've been through and regardless of what has happened in your life up to this point, a decision must be made by each of us to want a better world to live in and to treat each other better in order to really make a change in this world. The word enthusiasm means many things to many people. For some, when they hear the word enthusiasm they think of intense enjoyment or excitement. For me, it means the God from within. In other words, joy—plain and simple joy—the kind that just fills one up. Whether it's filling you up with so much excitement you can barely be in your own skin, or the quiet joy that just makes one's world perfect as it is.

I've always been told I have a lot of enthusiasm for life, and sometimes it's too much for people. I'm one of those individuals who people look at while walking by and wonder, "WHAT'S WRONG with her? Tone it down, lady!!" Usually, I'm just bouncing around on the clouds and full of energy. This is why I set out to understand enthusiasm—how people view the different levels of it, and why some seem to have a lack of it or are bothered by those who do show it. What about "my being" exemplifies this high level of enthusiasm to those around me? Mostly, I wanted to understand, and I searched for the answer to why some people appear to have no enthusiasm. Are they really lacking enthusiasm, or do they just not show it in a way most are accustomed to?

Earlier, I referenced the poem by Marianne Williamson, *"A Return to Love."* This poem impacted my life many years ago when I first read it. It helped me to realize the whole love vs. fear stance I have now. I recommend you find the poem and read it. That poem taught me the importance of enthusiasm and where it truly comes from. I learned that hiding behind all my fears and insecurities only made me more powerless and unavailable to others. I made myself "show up" or be present in the world. When I did, that gave me permission to love myself, my joy for life (or enthusiasm), and gave me the ability to see that same quality in others—even when others try to hide it. I used to read the entire poem every morning aloud (in first person) as a reminder of who I want to be and what I will allow in my life. Here is one part of the poem that still makes me emotional.

And, as we let our own light shine, we consciously give other people permission to do the same.

As we are liberated from our fear, our presence automatically liberates others.

Go liberate others. Each of us gets to be the beacon of hope and enthusiasm our world needs—one person at a time. As the famous movie title says "Pay It Forward." Bring some love, kindness and incredible energy back into our world. We are in this together, my friends. Our world is a beautiful place with wonderfully enthusiastic people just waiting to be loved and share their hearts. Let's all work together to be the difference makers, who one by one will make a huge impact and create change in our society that will ripple into our future generations. I encourage you to send me your stories of enthusiasm, love and joy to lionheartedliving@gmail.com and share the changes or impact you and your circle of influence have made in our world. When we conquer our fears, we change the energy and enthusiasm our world holds for us.

And if you're wondering, my son stayed! If you want to learn more about the lessons my sons and I learned as well as how enthusiasm can rock your world, follow me on my blog at choose2ooze.wordpress.com.

LJILJA HUBBARD *got her passion for life as a child through dance and the love of her generous immigrant parents. She and her brother were born and raised in the dairyland state of Wisconsin. Through dance and her family, she learned the importance of living life from one's heart and meeting people where they are. This outlook on life created the dedication Ljilja has for personal development and leadership.*

She is a single mother of two boys. Ljilja has worked at Merrill Lynch for a total of fourteen years where she has nurtured her love of lifelong learning and leadership skills. She has a BA in Technical Theatre from the University of Wisconsin-Stevens Point. Ljilja was blessed to do some professional theatre at the Utah Shakespearean Festival and South Coast Repertory Theatre. Here she learned that our world is just like the stage…we show people what we want them to see.

Ljilja is known for her kind and generous disposition as well as her love for the arts. She enjoys horseback riding, traveling, dancing, and being outdoors with her boys and family in her spare time.

CONTACT INFORMATION
lionheartedliving@gmail.com

6

I'm Glad I Did

Sheryl Isenhour

"Once a man, twice a child" has been said for many years, and it will continue to be a valid saying. When a child is born, it is dependent upon someone else for everything necessary to sustain life. As they grow and mature, they are then able to care for themselves and become a fully functional adult, but all too often, the adult will revert to childlike attitudes, actions, and inabilities to function independently of others. This is caused by natural aging, illnesses, and health conditions such as stroke, heart attack, dementia, and Alzheimer's disease, just to name a few.

Close relationships with family members are a gift and should not be taken for granted. When parents, relatives, or friends reach their elder years, they become even more precious. If time gives you the privilege of seeing your parents and family members reach their elder years, consider yourself one of the lucky ones. Some look at it as a chore rather than a chance to have time with them that many others do not get. They can have illnesses that require you to attend to them on a daily basis or a healthy body with a failing mind. You never know until the time comes what you will face with your loved ones. When we were young, taking care of our parents was not something that we thought about, but now the time is here.

Do you plan to keep them at home? Will you hire someone to take care of them, or will you place them in a facility? I had to make all of these decisions over the years, and I hope I can give you some insights. One thing you never want to say is "I wish I had."

I never knew that I would begin "raising parents" at the age of twelve and that it would last for over fifty years of my life. I took care of my parents, Jerry's parents, stepparents, and aunt and uncle.

It became a juggling act that I just accepted. Between full-time careers, marriage, children, homes, and aging parents, the balls added up one by one. I just kept tossing them in the air as my life filled up, praying they wouldn't come crashing down on my head.

Although the days were busy and the workload always growing, caring for my father was one of these wonderful experiences that taught me that life doesn't end when a person can no longer relate to what goes on around them. It is never easy to see the person we know slip into a world that only exists behind their eyes. They are breathing, their heart is beating, but in this moment and in our eyes, their mind is not working.

One Sunday morning my life took a drastic turn. Seconds would begin turning into minutes, minutes into hours, hours into days, days turned into weeks and weeks into months. This is how it went for me at the age of thirty-five.

I had just finished breakfast with my children when I got a call from my mother wanting me to come talk to my father. Now I don't know about you, but when I was young, this was never a good sign. This time was to be worse than anything I could have ever imagined.

I put the kids in the car and headed to their house. When I walked into the den, Dad was extremely pale and had cupped his face with his hands. I got down on my knees in front of him and pulled his fingers back. He was disoriented and didn't seem to realize I was even there. Finally, after calling out to him several times and asking what was wrong, he told me that his head hurt badly. Dad was never one to complain so I knew it was more than just a headache.

This was totally not like him. He was extremely intelligent and had a clarity about him that to me was almost superhuman. He never kept notes, but he never forgot anything, unlike most of us. He could do math faster in his head than I could do on a calculator. Actually, I never saw him use one. He would do quotes on house constructions in his head as I would add them on my calculator, and then he would wait for me to catch up with him before he would give me the total. I had often told him that I wished I had his mind. Now I look back and see how fast what you have can be taken away.

After realizing it was not within my powers to help Dad, I knew it was time to contact a doctor. Since it was Sunday I wasn't sure what to do. Did I call the doctor or take him to the hospital? Being from a small town and being friends with our family doctor, I had his personal number and decided to call him for assistance. I called and was relieved when I got an answer. He suggested that Dad and I meet him at the office. I immediately put my father into the car and made him as comfortable as possible. My mom did not think that there was a lot to worry about, and she chose to keep the kids with her at home, letting me take Dad alone.

We reached the office in about fifteen minutes, and by this time, Dad was bent double in the car, grasping his head with all his strength. It was hard for him to focus. His vision was blurry, and he was getting anxious. Alan helped me get him on the table at the office, and after only a few minutes, he explained that we needed to get to the hospital in Concord to run a test that he was not able to do at the office. We put Dad back into the car, and Alan followed us to the hospital. He had already informed them we were on the way, and they were waiting on us. We were taken directly in and immediately sent for a CT scan.

Shortly after the scan, Dad and I were put into an ambulance headed to Presbyterian Hospital in Charlotte. The only explanation was that they found some areas in the scan that they did not like. I called my mom and told her she should meet us there as soon as she could find someone to watch the kids. Time stood still in the ambulance. As I looked toward the back of the ambulance, they were putting IVs into Dad and doing what they could to calm him down. They looked at me, and I knew they wanted me to say something to him. They cut the siren off just long enough for me to speak loudly so that Dad could hear me, and I assured him that he was in good hands and I was there. I was near tears, wanting to get back there to him, but because of regulations, I had to stay strapped in. I felt so helpless.

Upon getting to the hospital, I was faced with people more worried about insurance than about the man lying on the stretcher. I know hospitals have rules, but where was the compassion? While I was frantically telling them that I had not had any time to get the paperwork, they were denying treatment to my father. Dr. Brawley, who was soon to be Dad's chief neurosurgeon, came in. He told everyone except me and his nurse to get out and leave us alone, and that he would take full responsibility for getting it worked out.

He talked with Dad for a few minutes, asked me a lot of questions, and told the nurses to get us upstairs for more scans and then to ICU. Again, we were bombarded with staff wanting to see insurance cards but in a much angrier tone. They were told to do what he said and to leave us alone.

This is when time sped up. Time was not our friend. I was informed that surgery was set for 6 AM the next morning. Mom got to the hospital about this time, and after bringing her up to speed, I went back to trying to comfort my father.

Visiting hours were over in ICU, and Mom said we ought to go home. This was not going to happen. I called my children, explaining to them how much I loved them but that I needed to stay with their grandfather. I asked Mom to have someone bring me some clean clothes in the morning and to make sure the children were taken care of. Mom left, and there was a sense of being totally alone as I curled up on a chair in the waiting room.

I could only spend so much time in the ICU with Dad, and the rest of the time I sat in the waiting room and prayed. I made several calls to the kids before bedtime to make sure they were okay and that they understood why I was not home. It never ceases to amaze me how children can understand when it's necessary. I didn't know how much they would have to take me at my word for the next several months.

Morning slowly came, and Dad's nurses and doctors began arriving. I was surprised and relieved that Dad was to have a full team of surgeons in the operating room with him. One doctor took his time to explain things a little more clearly to me while the others prepped for the surgery. They had located two aneurysms, one on either side of the brain, and since they were not able to cut the skull on both sides, they would have to open up where one was located and work their way around and through his brain to get to the other. Both were at the point of rupturing, and so there was no time to waste. Suddenly I was alone again, but I knew in my heart that Dad was in the best of hands.

They had taken Dad back early before anyone else had time to get there. My mother, brother, and grandmother got there shortly after they wheeled him into the operating room. Everyone began to pace the waiting room, but I just found a quiet corner and sat there. I needed to work out my emotions. I soon realized that someone was going to have to assume the strong position, and it did not take much time to realize it was going to have to be me.

Hours passed. Nurses would come out and assure us that the doctors were doing all they could do. Finally, Dr. Brawley slipped out for a minute only to tell us that they were nowhere near knowing the outcome of the surgery. He explained that he would not be back until it was over. He wanted to be there for my dad and me. That was all that mattered. For some unknown reason I was still calm. Did I know it was not his time to go?

After what seemed like an eternity, Dr. Brawley and several doctors came out. Dad, as they said, skirted death three different times during the surgery, and the next several hours would be critical. Again, time stood still. Hours later, they moved him back to the ICU unit that would be his home for the next fifteen weeks.

Night drew near, and again, I was going to have to make the choice of staying at the hospital or returning to my children. Over the next weeks, my kids and I would not have a lot of time together, so there had to be quality time. I made the decision not to bring them to the hospital for several weeks due to the bandages, Dad's lack of responsiveness, and the fact they were too young to go into ICU and could only see him through the window.

After continually staying at the hospital, except for the times I went home for a shower and a few minutes with the kids, they started letting me stay with Dad. I did not have to leave at the end of visiting hours as others did.

Several days passed before they let Dad wake up. Once awake, it was apparent that he did not know me as his daughter. He didn't remember anything that had happened. He knew none of the family. We were told that his memory should return in time, but there was no timeline to follow.

As he began to stay awake longer, he knew my name but not the person he associated with his daughter. But I would take whatever I was given. We became good "friends." I was the girl who helped him with what he needed.

I began taking care of many of my father's needs—bathing and feeding him—so the nurses could tend to the medical needs of other patients. Even though he did not know me as a daughter, we were getting closer, and he would talk to me and no one else. I became the communicator between him and the staff. Finally, he improved enough to get moved out of ICU, which posed a whole new series of problems. He was no longer sedated as much, and with his mental status where it was, he did not understand instructions. He still had a feeding tube, and there was no way that he was going to leave it alone. After pulling it out several times, they made the decision to restrain him. You have no idea how hard it is to watch a man be tied down. It is torture. Sometimes, I could talk him out of pulling it out during the day, but the night was not so easy. After he pulled it out several times and they had to replace it, his throat was getting raw. I decided the best thing was to sit beside his bed, tie his hands to mine, and sleep there. When he moved, I was able to wake up and take care of his needs, that is, if I went to sleep at all.

He grew more coherent now that he was not sedated, and we began having some long conversations about the time he thought he was living in. The past was clear. The present was only the moment we were in at any second. We spent a lot of time back in World War II, discussing what was going on there. At times, I was a nurse, and at other times, I was one of the people in his platoon. I was whatever he needed me to be at that moment.

At other times, we were building houses. Dad had built houses from the time he left the army until the day we ended up at the hospital. One day, Dr. Brawley walked in when I was standing across Dad in the center of the bed, swinging my arms upward. I was asked what, if I didn't mind him asking, I was doing. Dad quickly said, "She is hanging sheetrock, and if you will shut up, she can finish." Dr. Brawley chuckled and shook his head. He said it amazed him that I would do whatever it took to keep Dad calm. But what else did I have to do?

Many days when I needed a break or wanted a few minutes to read the medical books the nurses had brought on how the brain works, I would pretend to knock over the nail bucket, and he was content as long as I sat on the floor to pick them up.

Another day, the doctor walked into the room with Dad getting ready to strike a lighter, not a problem except for the oxygen he was on. After Dr. Brawley nearly had a heart attack, I told him not to worry. It wouldn't light, didn't even have a striker. You see, my dad had smoked all his life, and now he had been operated on, tied up, lost his dignity and more, I had decided that he should be able to think he could smoke.

I had stopped at the store that morning after going home for clean clothes and picked up a lighter, a carton of cigarettes, straws exactly the size of cigarettes, some glue, scissors and a razor blade. I cut the bottom of the box open, then the bottom of the cigarette packs and removed the cigarettes. I replaced them with straws cut to the exact length of his cigarettes and stuffed them with cotton so they would not bend. I glued the packs shut and then the box. I placed the carton back into the bag from the store, along with the lighter with no fluid or striker, and gave them to him. The excitement I saw in his face made me keep this up for the remainder of his stay. I left the hospital with two Ziploc bags full of "cigarettes" when his stay was over. I would not dare reuse the straws since the box and packs would not look perfect. But what else did I have to do?

Once they removed the feeding tube and he could eat real food, we spent many meals and many hours with "a bite for you, a bite for me." By this time, the nurses were bringing me food from the cafeteria so I could work with Dad to get him to eat. I was doing most of the daily care other than changing IVs and giving meds.

Dad was having alternating good and bad days, but at least he was alive and we could work with that. We had been in ICU for fifteen weeks, and now we were headed toward our tenth week in a regular room. They had taken him off IVs and put him on oral meds. The powers that be were at the point of kicking him out of the hospital. Not sure what it would be like with him at home, Mom began preparing the house for his release from the hospital.

He still did not know Mom, my brother, or me. Over the past weeks, he had been telling them he did not know who they were, and he wanted them to leave. Needless to say, I was not one of their favorite people since he was telling them I was the only one he wanted there. Such is life.

The day before they were to release him, he had this strange look on his face. He looked at me in a way I had not seen over the last twenty-five weeks. He called me by name and asked how Lori and David, rather Cute and Hardrock, his grandchildren, were doing. Tears began to flow, and even though Dad did not know why, he cried with me.

The time came to leave. We packed up our things, and Dad, Mom and I headed down the road toward home. Dad still did not recognize my mother, which made the ride rather long. She did not understand why he didn't know her. As we pulled out of the parking lot onto the road, my dad began screaming to pull over. I steered to the side of the road to see what was happening, and he was shaking. I asked him what was wrong, and he just kept saying we were going to hit something. I assured him we were not, and we pulled back onto the road again, for him just to resume the screaming. Mom was in the back screaming at him because he was screaming. So we stopped once again. Not sure of what was going on, I convinced Dad to put his hands over his eyes and lay his head back. Several times on the way home, he would remove his hands, and we would go through it again.

I was never so happy to see their driveway. I was sure life was headed back to normal now, but it wasn't to be so. We pulled up in front of the house, and Dad turned to me and asked, "Who lives here?" Unable to convince him that he was home, I told them to stay in the car and I would be right back. I opened the door to the house and went in. Upon my return a minute later, I told him that the owners of the house had suggested that we stay there for a few days until he was stronger. It was hard to convince Mom to play the game, but finally, she had no choice and went along with it.

After getting Dad settled and fixing them some lunch, I proceeded to finish making the house ready for Dad to move around. The evening went on, and I noticed that when Dad had to go to the bathroom, he headed in the wrong direction. Then when he went to the bedroom to lie down, he did the same. This concerned me, but I had an idea I wanted to explore. After he had had a good nap, I sat down beside him and asked him if he could draw the floor plan to his house. In the years prior to his surgery, we had spent many hours drawing floor plans that he would use to build spec houses. I gave him a piece of paper, and he drew the house totally inverted from the one we were sitting it. It was then that I realized what was right for most of us was left to him, thus his fear of cars being on the wrong side of the road on the way home.

Dad had been home for several days when one morning he woke up and headed in the right direction. The mind had put right and left back into their place. The next day he remembered my mother and several days after that, my brother. We were on our way to a semi-normal life again. Dad never got all his short-term memory back, and he never regained any memories from that Sunday morning when it all started until after he was home for over a week. This remained a total void in his memory. But I did have memories, wonderful but hard memories. Another thing that I had now was a time in his life that he and I could talk about–the army. We had things to talk about that he had never told anyone else. This had been a time in his life that he refused to talk about with my mother or anyone else.

I think I was given this time to get to know the man I admired more than anyone else in the world. These are the times you treasure.

After making it through all this, Dad was not to live but a few more years. He was diagnosed with Stage IV cancer and passed away in six short weeks after diagnosis, but that is another story.

It's because of times like these that I coach people to know that the bad times can be their best times. Life has its way of turning disaster into something marvelous. Do not feel sorry for me, but rejoice that I was given the time to get to know my father and say the things that I needed to say that would one day be forever lost to death.

I became a coach, a trainer and a public speaker to let people know that they do not have to go through these times alone. If I had had someone to talk to during this time, and others that followed, it would have helped me to understand that what I was going through was not just my journey but one that others had taken, also. Therefore, one of the avenues I have chosen to coach and train in the field of is taking care of aging parents. You see, this was just the beginning of my raising parents. After marrying Jerry and acquiring his parents, stepparents, aunt, and uncle, I had many more experiences. Before becoming an empty nester at sixty-two, I had experienced the single parenting of my two children, aneurysms, cancer, heart attacks, diabetes, dementia, Alzheimer's, alcoholism, and just plain old age. I had full-time businesses while doing this, and with it all going on, my immediate family turned out great. The juggling act became a normal part of life, and I do not regret any ball that I juggled.

Life makes many turns, but how you deal with them is what makes it special. The realization is that you do not have to do it alone.

You want to be able to say "I'm glad I did" instead of "I wish I had."

Thank you for taking your time to read one of my stories. As you make your journey, I wish each of you will realize you are not alone. Remember the past, enjoy the present, and look to the future with hope.

SHERYL ISENHOUR *has been known as the problem solver and go-to person her whole life. She has been a single mother of two children. She has nursed and cared for elderly parents, both her own and her in-laws, until they passed. She developed her drive and inner strength doing everything from becoming the caretaker of her mother and their home at the age of twelve to surviving personal and business trials. She test-ed the male-dominated fields, from driving semis and limos to building a wallcovering business in times when women were supposed to stay at home. She has been an active participant and keeper of the books in multiple successful family businesses. She built two successful businesses prior to becoming CEO of a successful outdoor living manufacturer, IBD Outdoor Rooms. In that role, she has proven herself to be an accomplished designer and a recognized expert in the field of outdoor furniture and living areas. Through her talks, inspiration and assistance, she has coached others to find success in their own life goals and pursuits, and she might just be the resource you need when your dreams seem out of reach!*

Tom Ziglar, head of Ziglar Coaching and one of Sheryl's coaches, says, "Sheryl Isenhour is proving to be one of our most valued Ziglar Legacy Certi-fied trainers and coaches. She showed intense interest in adopting the training associated with her certification as both trainer and one-on-one success coach, growing our confidence in her commitment. We realize the Ziglar standard for legacy trainers and coaches is unique to the industry, and it's rewarding and encouraging to have Sheryl represent the Ziglar brand. She offers her own professional style of integrating the Ziglar philosophy with her delightful per-sonality and ability to identify with others. Our confidence in Sheryl Isenhour is surpassed only by her heartfelt desire to contribute to the lives of those she touches with the timeless message."

Life has a way of presenting each of us with failures. You know, those roadblocks that block our travels to our dreams when life so often throws a curveball. Sheryl lives by the John Maxwell creed of always falling forward, turning failures into successes, time after time in her own life, and she helps others when they face these challenges. As Vince Lombardi shared, "The winner is the person who gets up when they are knocked down." She is a winner who has been known all her life as the one to help others get back up after they have been knocked down! That true grit comes from the person who inspired her in life…her father!

In this life-long process, Sheryl has learned the delicate art of balancing one's professional life with the duties and responsibilities of one's family life. She did it, when at an all too young age, she faced her father's declining health as he battled aneurisms and eventually lost to cancer. She overcame her own business and personal obstacles and turned them into success stories. Some may say she is a survivor, but in reality, she is a creative problem solver who works tirelessly and persistently to make things happen and remove roadblocks to success. In other words, she has already done what many spend their lives hoping to accomplish. Remarkably, she keeps giving to others without expectations of rewards!

Sheryl has a true gift in her ability to assist people with their challenges, that sacred duty of taking care of parents, her husband's parents and other family members as they age. She has dealt personally with the issues of dementia, Alzheimer's disease, alcoholism, heart issues, aneurisms and cancer, along with the emotional issues that are associated with the problems of aging loved ones. She understands this journey is easier if you have someone there to help guide you through some of these problems and will be there for you. Unless this person has faced these issues personally, it is hard for them to really provide that help so often needed, you see she understands what you are feeling!

She also understands the challenges that working with your family in business present to your personal life. She has walked the walk, so she can talk the talk. Having worked with husbands, children and other family members, she understands the difficulty so many face in making the required decisions in business that must be made while not disrupting the family unit. A tall order, but one she has experienced and one she continues to build her skills to coach on.

You know the feeling; we all get it at times. The wall is up, it blocks your path. The challenges of life and the stress that is carried from your business life *hover over you like a storm that will not blow away. It blocks your happiness at home with your loved ones and the ability to take care of your responsibilities. Sheryl understands, but more than that Sheryl can share with you the processes to get past the obstacles that block your path and hinder you from reaching your dreams. Today her passion and motivation is to bring her attitude, experience, and deep knowledge of business and life to the service of others. It is her joy to help others be successful in every phase of their life. This ability has been enhanced along the way in such high-powered training courses as the Zig Ziglar Legacy Certification and Ziglar Coaching Certification. But, as Sheryl will tell you, her greatest teacher has been life, and the business of life itself.*

Feel free to contact her at (704) 425-0211 or via email at sheryl@cvclifecoaching.com. She can answer any additional questions and determine if she is the right person for you or your company.

For more information on Sheryl Isenhour's coaching, speaking and seminars, visit sherylisenhour.com or call 704-425-0211.

7

Moldy Me
Dean Mahlstedt

Mold Crisis at Home

1998 was the year that Lorna and I purchased a fifteen-year-old cleaning and restoration business in the small town where we both grew up. Having been in the cleaning, inspection, and remediation business now for eighteen years, I have been exposed to the reality that we all can be blind to innovation and solutions that would benefit us if we only knew they existed and that we could trust those people connected to those solutions. The vast amount of information that is available on the Internet can lead us all on wild goose chases for that solution we are so desperate to find when we need to fix or figure out something.

The issue of mold contamination in homes and the workplace is no exception. Many, including my wife and me, have spent countless hours on the web searching for answers about mold and its effect on our health. Which information can we believe? Who has the most credibility? What studies and research are available to prove what is true about mold in homes and the work place? If I see mold in my home, what do I do to clean it up? We always seem to feel sick or cough or have headaches when we spend time in our house. Is our house making us sick? So many stories, so many experts, so many documents, so many rabbit trails to continually cause any of us to question our sanity and the valid-ity of what anyone is saying about mold.

For many years, our company participated in the"spray to kill"mold remediation protocols. Many battles have been fought to determine if mold is a real health threat or simply a visual nuisance in our lives. So much politics and greed has infected the battles over the years. Fortu-nately, the standard of care has changed, whereby we now know that "killing"the mold can cause greater problems. Mold removal is the key. In 2012, our family was shocked into a new reality when my wife went through a sudden decline in health that was ultimately diagnosed as Lyme disease and additionally mold sensitivity, both of which attacked her immune system with brute biological force. She was the first one to inquire of me if we possibly had a mold issue in our home. My quick, initial response was to deny the possibility. I was wrong.

A very simple investigation took place over a short time. This includ-ed moving my nightstand to reveal mold growing on an exterior wall at the northwest corner of our bedroom—right where we slept! I employed moisture metering of certain areas of our house, followed by moving some more furniture, and then the water heater, then some minor sur-gical style demolition, and finally a full demolition of the lower level of our home and part of the main level as well. But wait! I am a cleaning and restoration professional! How could this happen under my watch? Much pride had to be set aside on my part so that our family could begin the long journey that would eventually bring healing to our health and our home.

Within a short amount of time after Lorna's diagnosis, we tested and were informed that I had Lyme/mold health issues and so did eight of our nine children. A season of discovery was upon our family. Lorna studied technical documents on medicine, health and nutrition while I dove headfirst into building science documents to answer the questions: Why did this happen to our home? How do I repair our home so that it will be mold proof? Is there such a thing as mold proof? How do I change the way we remediate and repair client homes?

The Internet was a key tool that enabled us to discover, learn, vet, and practice our newfound knowledge of mold, water damaged buildings, natural vs commercial medicine, nutrition, and mold avoidance. We decided that it would be beneficial for me to travel extensively to receive training, meet other building science and indoor air quality professionals, and participate in retreats. We even attended a multi-day medical professional conference as a couple so that we could put up our best fight to win back our health and home. We spent nearly four intense years from 2012 to 2016 on this mission.

Since that time, most of the members of our family have been cleared of Lyme and related co-infections, and most mold issues, although we must maintain a mold avoidance watch for our health to remain in a positive state. We have also been able to completely change the way our company provides both water and mold remediation and have employed better protections for our employees and for the occupants of homes we work in. In all of this, we can take no credit for ourselves. We have deep faith and convictions about God and our faith in Jesus Christ that carried us and our burdens through all of this and still carries us today.

Helping Others Through Their Crises

With all this new knowledge and success in healing and building science came a passion to help others who were suffering the same, or worse, than what we had experienced. I take most of the indoor air quality calls, and Lorna often volunteers her time with other women who are at their wits end, experiencing similar negative health impacts themselves or in their families. The stories are heart wrenching as we spend time with families that are plagued with illness and are financially strained or ruined due to mold contamination. The resulting negative health issues are burdensome. We see professionals who were very successful people when they were healthy. Some are forced to leave work because of new physical limitations. Even children who have been affected by mold become disconnected from school and normal activities as their immune systems are overloaded by exposures to toxins.

Many of the people that we meet are looking for the "golden" answer and a reprieve from their financial or medical agonies. We have been in their shoes. We know how it feels. We understand the moments and days of hopeless desperation. The "golden" answer does not yet exist. We have learned how to mitigate against poor health and how to properly assess and repair buildings damaged by water and mold, although there is much more to learn. Our company is providing more and more investigation, consulting, and testing, which raises questions of how to best serve clients who are being negatively affected by issues in their homes or workplaces.

The challenge is how to get information to clients and how to keep that information timely and relevant. A tremendous amount of change takes place in the Indoor Air Quality industry each year concerning mold and other indoor contaminates. The Institute of Inspection Cleaning Restoration Certification has the most recognized standard of care for mold remediation (IICRC S520). An important predecessor documented standard of care is the IICRC S500 Water Damage Remediation Standard. Another certification standard is the Restoration Industry Association Certified Mold Professional (CMP). The EPA, CDC, WHO, individual states, and other nations have their own documents dealing with mold in buildings and mold effects on human health.

On the medical side of this issue, there are several medical doctors, natural health professionals, and even dentists who are researching the impact of mold indoors and treating patients with mold related illnesses. The Global Indoor Health Network is one of the newest and best clearing houses with resources and research documents on mold related illnesses. I can fill up two pages with links to various resources which represent thousands of pages of information. When forwarded to a client, they can lose hope and wither at the prospect of having to endure hours or days of research to learn about mold and what to do to fix their mold problems.

Caveat Venditor and Caveat Emptor – Let the Seller and Buyer Beware

A typical phone call from a client about mold begins with a general inquiry about what services we provide and the cost of services. Behind those two questions is often a set of deeper and more meaningful questions that most do not even know to ask. Because our family has dealt with mold issues in our home and in our personal health, it has become protocol to answer their inquiry with a series of questions about their home and their health. A few homeowners push back because they are simply comparing our services and pricing against others who they have called and/or are attempting to qualify or disqualify our usefulness to their situation.

Many of these types of callers have already been down a fruitless journey with other investigators, remediation professionals, medical doctors or agencies that have cost them real money and often they have come away empty handed with no answers (and less money in the bank). Others engage and quickly answer my questions as they are eager to stumble upon the possibility that their home is making them sick, or that for the first time in their quest someone is finally asking relevant questions to match what they have been wondering about their home and their health.

Likewise, an investigation at the home or business of a client elicits many different responses. Many men deny that mold is an issue or question that the tools we use to diagnose building issues are accurate. Others believe we have meters that detect and/or identify mold. We do not. They do not yet exist, but we do anticipate their development and arrival. Both men and women sometimes "forget" to tell us about all/any of the past water damage events that have taken place in their home or business. This is important material evidence that helps diagnose indoor air quality problems and potential locations of mold colonization. Some "forget" because they are embarrassed by these past events because they think they will look foolish or irresponsible.

Men of sudden expertise like to "assist" at investigations to show exactly where the problems are and instruct us that we need not look any farther than that area. We have clients who have a lot of "stuff" that adds to mold issues and impedes investigation. Finally, some have pen and paper in hand and simply follow, ask questions, write down answers, and ask more questions until they have enough information to make good decisions. Many similarities exist between buildings that we inspect for mold and water damage, but each one can be different and would be difficult to diagnose over the phone.

It is common to spend up to two hours on the phone answering and asking questions. On-site investigation can take from three to six hours, inspecting mold damaged homes where occupants are experiencing negative health effects. Sampling may, or may not, be performed, which can add a couple more hours of field and administration time after the initial phone call and inspection. The information and resources that are shared during the process can be overwhelming. In some cases, difficult decisions about personal belongings, pets, treatments, medical decisions and even career/job changes must be made. There are many investigations where I wish I was a counter attendant at an ice cream shop and had just handed the family their last delicious ice cream cone. I would rather have become a small hero in their day, rather than the Grim Reaper.

However, these circumstances and the reality of health and money issues typically cause me to reveal facts that need to be shared with these families. This type of revelation can be cause for many new emotions and decisions on the part of the affected clients, about their homes and potentially their workplaces. In our case, the decisions (for the affected owners of a restoration company) were not easy, even when considering the resources available at ProCare to provide repairs to our own home. While it is true that we have tools and expertise to deal with losses of many types, the burden to provide repairs, regain our family health, and transform the protocols of how we deal with others and their homes is no easier burden than anyone else we have met. I can say with much satisfaction and relief that our family has come through this stormy season much stronger, healthier, and with more wisdom than we had before.

Caveat Lector – Let the Reader Beware

As we continue to take apart wet and moldy homes, this nation has seen the construction of millions of homes that have a great potential to fail when a water loss event, storm, or extreme weather condition takes place. The types of primary building materials made available by manufacturers, coupled with the building codes, will undoubtedly cause countless more homes and occupants to be negatively impacted by mold and other microbial contaminates, resulting in people (and even their pets) becoming ill. Many of these people will not find immediate relief because they will not make the connection that their health issues may be caused by their home or workplace environments. Many more will seek professional medical help and find themselves frustrated, not heard, incorrectly diagnosed, and placed on treatment protocols that do not address the core issues. The medical profession is still largely blind to the effects of today's failing buildings and materials on occupant health, but a few brave souls have risked reputation to research and develop relevant treatment protocols. At the same time, we are blessed to see a growing element of people from all walks of life who are bringing mold-related experiences and their own stories into public view to collaborate with others and facilitate solutions for moldy environments and occupants.

We believe that the information and protocols for mold remediation and health treatments will continue to improve as professionals and lay people alike push research and results into the public sphere. Major change as to how we build, or retrofit, our homes is desperately needed. An attitude change is required and reprioritizing of values in our society. Our abundance of "stuff" and our lack of care/training in maintaining and building healthy homes are to our own detriment. In this industry, as in others, greed and politics do enter as causal agents that can impede progress. Without broad-based change in the building codes and available materials, new homes will continue to be built that will fail to provide a healthy indoor environment for the homeowners and likewise for some commercial buildings.

The problems that arise from moldy buildings can and will be overcome by the growing group of people who have successfully remediated and regained their health, by those who are in the middle of the fight, and by researchers who continue to discover solutions for all of us to employ and share with those in need. In our work, I am often reminded about the well-known starfish story where the old man is walking on the beach as the sun gains and the tide recedes. He is found by a young man who sees him throwing stranded starfish back into the sea. When challenged as to the effectiveness of his mission and the fact that many starfish would remain stranded and die by days' end, the old man replies, "It made a difference to that one." The parallel of that man to Christ, who seeks and saves us, is what keeps me going to help others make it back to a safe place. ▪

DEAN MAHLSTEDT *lives in rural Minnesota with his wife Lorna and their nine children. Since 1998 they have owned and operated ProCare Service, Inc, a thirty-four-year-old cleaning, inspection and restoration company. Dean has been certified in Critical Incidence Stress Management, became trained and certified to provide trauma scene clean-up and has held various cleaning and restoration certifications through the IICRC. Most recently, he worked through the three-level Restoration Industry Association Certified Mold Professional Certification Program and is number forty of forty-one certified to this level. Additional training with Wonder Makers Environmental for Mold Sensitized Individuals and attendance at the Surviving Mold Arizona doctors' conference enhance his investigations and approach to mold-sensitized clients. The Mahlstedt family enjoys being with friends, traveling, and playing bluegrass and gospel music.*

Dean can be reached by contacting the ProCare office, 320-286-5748 or by email. dean@procaremn.com. Please visit the ProCare website at www.procaremn.com.

8

It Is Okay to Be Beautiful
A Note to Self

Andrea Meilleur

I am here today because I need to tell you about what I have learned, in hopes that it will change your future into something wonderful. The very first thing I want to tell you is that you are going to be okay. I can assure you that it is okay to be beautiful and still be safe. As we sit here on this funky seventy's green couch in our tiny one-bedroom home, I feel the comfort and pride it brought in providing this safe place for our little girl. If you look around this little house, you will note what a gift it is. You have good neighbors to watch over you while being in a location perfect for this time in your life. You are doing well, and it is going to get better.

Why Has Everything Been So Painful?

The past pain is supplying the strength that you are going to need in your future. Remember when you were twelve? Please try to understand it was neither your fault, nor something you did. It was that powerful force that exploded outward as you took the most powerful stand you had ever taken for yourself, making you feel strong. Remember how he stood up, held his chin, and how the blow was never felt on your hand? The fear and adrenalin that shot through your body was felt as you quickly stumbled home for comfort only to hear the crushing words alluding to your blame. Then the years of criticism and shame that followed pouring out from your supposed protectors, destroying your self-esteem. It created so much confusion as to what was right and what was wrong. Along with a lack of connection and understanding about love—ultimately leading you into positions where a punch would not have made a difference in the outcome. Often, you have been told how beautiful you are, but it seemed it was mostly from those who wanted to take advantage of you.

You must pay close attention and focus on the strength inside of you. The courage of a lion that it took to stand up for yourself. This is the strength that you are going to need to get you through many challenges that are coming. Your future holds relationships where things will not go so well. However, the three beautiful children to come will rock your world. What you need is in you this very moment, and you are perfect exactly as you are. You are gaining the wisdom, knowledge, and strength to protect yourself and your children. The only reason you have this incredible strength is because of what you endured in the past.

The people in your life who are hurting you right now are victims, too. Your family has set you up to feel worthless and useless only because that is how they feel about themselves. You will find you can change no one, only yourself. Whatever your mind focuses on is what you are going to attract into your life. It is okay for you to think of yourself as being beautiful, important, and needed. All this growing is going to allow you to become a better wife, mother, and leader in the future. But for now, you need to be strong for your children.

Your first marriage is going to be very challenging, and the best way to handle it is to allow yourself to be happy. You already know how priceless your beautiful two-year-old daughter is. Once the two girls and boy are added, your life is going to be running over with joy.

How Can I Be a Good Mother When I Have No Clue?

The truth is you will figure it out. Nobody knows how to do it perfectly, and no one else has ever been the mother of your children. One of the most important things that you can do for your children is to love yourself and feel worthy of achieving your dreams. A mentally healthy mother will create happy and mentally healthy children.

I want you to see how this little girl is so loving and beautiful. You feel so much joy in your heart with her now. Just wait until you see her grow up and become a mother! It is imperative for you to love yourself so that you can teach self-love, and she can teach her children to do the same. Everything you think and feel is going to affect your precious children, forever.

In the future, your children are going to get on your last nerve, but you need to love every second you have with them. They are the greatest gift you will ever have. There will many rocky roads ahead with them, and remember a handbook has not been provided. Make laughter the song of your home, and spend focused quality time with them. You must strive to do more with them every day because in twenty-five years they are all going to be moved out and you are going to miss them so much it will hurt. Live in every moment, and do as much as you can to make them laugh and smile right now.

Teach your children about gratitude at a deeper level, even with the small things. Remember they are listening to what you say to others and about others. What you feel about yourself is very loud and gets imprinted on them. Award them with being happy with their true selves. Teach them to be beautiful souls, to be grateful, and to know that they have everything they need already built inside of them. They each have precious gifts they will give to others. You are not going to do everything right the first time. It is a part of learning—keep trying. If one thing does not work, try another way.

How Can I Feel Worthy When I Feel So Useless and Dirty?

You made a decision when you were about seventeen years old to never expect anything good so you could no longer be disappointed by life. By focusing on the negative, you became more negative. Start focusing on the positive and the good. Since you are going to be telling yourself something anyway, say something good. I am enough! I am worthy! I am beautiful! I am lovable! I am important! I am valuable to everyone around me! These are just a few to get started with.

It is very important to start growing yourself immediately from this day forward. You want to set up habits that you do every morning and every night without fail. Start reading books now! Even if it means you read three pages a night. Remember how Uncle Freeman told you to start saving a quarter a day to save enough for a down payment on a car? Well, you didn't do it and wished you had. This must be different. You are going to build and build, just by reading those three pages a day. Since you are very interested in finance, it is the perfect place to start. You can find a lot of books that will teach you about it. In the future, you will have more information than you ever dreamed of at your fingertips in an instant. Continue to use this to grow yourself.

No matter what, START NOW! Love yourself and others unconditionally. Always insist on respect. It is okay to stay away from people who do not help you grow. It is easier than you think to separate yourself from those who do not have the welfare of your family in mind. The benefits far outweigh the challenges you will encounter in the beginning as you make this a part of your new standards.

In order for you to be open to giving to others, you should start with forgiveness. That means everyone, including you. You have done the best with what you know. It is not about you doing everything right or wrong. It is about what you learn and what will grow you. You cannot change others, so you should see them as they are and accept them. Understand they are on their own journey they need to figure out. The most powerful thing that you can do now is change yourself.

It is time to feel wonderful about who you are. Dress in what makes you feel beautiful. You are a beautiful soul inside and out; this is a good thing to feel. Do not ever forget how you feel about yourself and others is how your children will view the world. Remain grateful for every little thing around you. Creating your own happiness will help you to stay happy even when things are not going so well.

Every challenge of every day you have been given was designed for you to give back in the future. Although it has been painful, you have learned some valuable lessons. You have gained strength that you will need in your future. You have not yet realized the things you are capable of. The compelling drive inside is going to propel you to heights yet not seen. Keep it alive! It will take you further than you can even imagine. At this point, it does not seem like it will pay off, but it will!

How Can I Accomplish Big Things in The Future When No One Believes In Me?

What other people think about you does not define who you are. First, realize you are exactly perfect the way you are right this moment, and this will open so many doors for you. You never caused the people to mistreat you. It was of their own accord. The cruel incidences gave you an instinct to protect your children from dangerous people. The way you define those situations will make a difference about who you let in your life. Everything in life is a lesson. There is something for you to learn and something to help you go forward. It is nothing more, and it does not determine your worth. If you just look at what has worked and what has not worked, you will get so much more from it. It is imperative that you find people to surround yourself with who are positive and authentic.

There are some things that if changed now will change the course of your children's futures. First, you must forgive yourself. You did not do any of this stuff on purpose. It just happened. For some people, what happened to you would be horrible, and they would not even fathom it. There are also other people who would say it would be the least of their problems as they have had much worse things happen to them. You have lived the best you could with the information you have had. I want you to realize you are perfect as you are.

How Can I Possibly Forgive?

Forgiving those who are hurting you now seems impossible, but it can be done. They have their own stories and monsters in the closet you are not aware of. It does not mean you should let them in—keep them out and separate from them. When you start focusing on and looking for people who love themselves—hard workers and the positive thinkers—you will find them.

I Have Heard This Before. What Does It Mean?

I now know the answer to that question. It means that you do not entertain any negativity, or negative people, not even negative entertainment. Instead, fill your mind with visions of the things you are so thankful for. When you wake up in the morning, be thankful for the beautiful day even if it is raining! Take in the beauty of the sunshine and notice that even breathing is such a blessing.

How Can I Change My Life to Make It Work Out Better?

The very first thing to do is start picking out things that you are grateful for. Even the things that have hurt you in your life, you can be grateful for. Start daily habits. Next, you need to remember to surround yourself with people who are positive, loving, and believe in your big dreams. Use your intuition, and if something does not feel right or you do not feel good when you are around someone, do not spend any time with them.

Be sure to always dress in your best clothes, and make yourself look good and feel good. Do not expect anyone else to make you feel good. Make yourself feel good! Love what you see in the mirror. Love it because you are beautiful! Surround yourself with the things that make you feel joyful. You already have picked up eating habits that are healthier. Keep exploring those, and always look for other ideas outside of the area where you live. There is a whole big world out there, and you do not have to be afraid of it. Whatever happens in life ask yourself: *What is life trying to teach me?* Do not think of it as right or wrong, just look for life's lessons.

• • •

From a very young age and on past my fortieth birthday, I struggled with depression and low self-esteem. It took that long for life to turn around again and put me in a place to help my twenty-year-old self. The unthinkable things I have been through knocked me down again and again, but I never stopped getting back up. Now I do not take no for an answer, and I do not allow myself to feel bad.

Abuse of any kind is unacceptable. It includes emotional, physical, and sexual abuse. Most people are aware that physical and sexual abuse also leaves deep emotional scars, and it must be stopped. What gets less attention are the situations in which people call you names, make fun of you, or threaten you. Never allow them in your life, no matter who they are.

I promise you can look and feel beautiful and still be safe.

ANDREA MEILLEUR *is a mother, wife, speaker, coach, and entrepreneur. She has four children, five grandchildren, and is married to the love of her life. She earned her Bachelor's degree in Business Administration at McKendree University in 2010 after getting her girls through college. A devoted grandmother by day and a writer by night, her passion is to inspire and make people laugh. Not a regular laugh but a deep, full belly laugh! Her goal is to teach people, no matter where they might be in life, to become their best selves—while always remembering to help others more than herself.*

CONTACT INFORMATION
Andrea Meilleur
andrea.meilleur17@gmail.com

9

Healing From Cancer
Forever Changed For the Good

Lyn Schneidermann

On August 31, 2016, I received a phone call from my doctor that forever changed my world. She said she was sorry, but the tests had come back positive, that I had cancer. I will always remember the place where I received that phone call. My husband, Kevin, and I were sitting on a bench by the lake. Beautiful, peaceful scenery in front of me, my world that I knew was crashing down around me. I politely thanked my doctor and kept my composure until we ended the call, then I broke down and cried while my husband held me and cried with me.

After I regained my composure Kevin prayed for guidance and direction for what we would be facing. Then we had to tell our family the news. We were attending a conference with our daughter for the week, and our three sons were back home. How do you tell someone this kind of news? We didn't really know what we were dealing with at this point. As our sons were working, we decided to call them that evening when they were all together. We texted our daughter and asked her to meet us by the lake when her session was done. We then called our parents to tell them and texted our siblings to let them know. I had a biopsy the week before, so they all knew I would be finding out the results that week. My sister called me right away, and we talked and cried together. Our daughter came a while later, and we told her and shed a few tears again. That evening we called our sons and told them. That was really hard to tell them when we were hundreds of miles away, and I couldn't see their faces to see how they were doing or to give them a hug.

The next day I texted our children this verse and message to them, "Trust in the LORD with all thine heart and lean not on your own understanding, but in all your ways acknowledge Him and He shall direct your path. Proverbs 3:5-6." I also told them this did not take God by surprise. He knew this would happen to me before I was even born. We need to trust Him with all this, and He has it under control. This verse became our motto to cling to when we did not know where this would end up or what direction to go. At the conference, someone was selling calligraphy, and we found the verse of Proverbs 3:5-6. We bought it, and it hangs above my dresser to remind me every day that I need to trust God and not myself.

I received a call from the cancer center the next day to set up an appointment with the cancer team the following week. It all seemed so surreal and scary, and at the same time I didn't know how serious this cancer was. We finished the conference and went home and spent time as a family praying together and shedding a few tears as the reality was setting in that I had cancer.

On Sunday, we attended church, and Kevin asked for prayers for me and what we would be facing. No one knew that I had had any testing done, so it was a shock to our church family. My dear husband was a bit teary eyed as he shared the news up front that his wife had cancer. It is interesting how people react when you tell that kind of news. Most people were supportive, but some avoided me. It seemed they didn't know what to say or how to react.

I was beginning to process how I got this cancer. I had purposely taken steps to help prevent cancer as cancer runs in my family. My mom had cancer twice; her mom and her sisters had cancer; and my dad also had cancer. Not the greatest of odds for me, so I had purposed to change things in my life to help prevent me from getting cancer. I had nursed all my children, changed my diet to organic when available, and used natural medicine for many years. I had also had all my mercury fillings removed. The dentist replaced one of the fillings with a gold crown instead of a porcelain one, but all the other fillings were replaced with porcelain. Most of my fillings were from when I was a little girl. I also used a natural hormone replacement therapy instead of the synthetic one. So, I thought I had all my bases covered, but I also knew I had been struggling with issues with my digestive system over the last few years.

The following Thursday we met with the cancer team. The cancer center assigns you a team of doctors—just for you. The team included the oncologist, surgeon, radiation oncologist, and the genetics counselor. We met with the oncologist first. His job was to determine during surgery how much the surgeon was to remove depending on what the cells showed as he examined them. He did not like to be asked questions. He came across as arrogant, and he had all the answers and I knew nothing. I was told this cancer was estrogen receptor and progesterone receptor positive cancer. I had asked him how I could have gotten this cancer as I was using a natural progesterone. I knew breast cancer was usually estrogen dominant, and I tried to take preventatives to avoid this. He told me that progesterone supplementation causes cancer. I tried asking him how this is, but he brushed off my questions and left the room. Not exactly a doctor with a good bedside manner!

The surgeon came in next and was not much better than the oncologist. He explained what he would do and how the oncologist would assist to make sure they got all the cancer cells. It seemed like he just saw me as a number, and he really wasn't very personable either. We didn't bother to ask any questions. The radiation oncologist came in next and explained what he would be doing and what I would go through during the four weeks of radiation. He was the most personable of the three doctors and explained to us about my tumor. My tumor, as I did know, was the size of a walnut and was hormone receptor positive and was invasive and at a Stage 2. Invasive means some cells were outside of the tumor and the tumor was not contained, but the cancer itself was slow growing. We liked this doctor the best and felt comfortable with him. He also told me that the goal was to make it to five years, so I could get my five-year survival pin. Those words hit me hard. It made me realize I might not be alive in five years.

By this time, about three hours had passed, and all the information was getting overwhelming. We were meeting with a nurse by this time to set up a time for the surgery. They wanted us to make a decision that day to do the surgery within a few weeks. We told them we needed to process all this information, and we were not going to schedule surgery at this time. They told me I could wait a month to decide. I knew that would be fine as this cancer was slow growing.

We ended up meeting with the genetics counselor a few weeks later, who wanted me to do blood work testing to determine if my cancer was genetic since breast cancer runs on my mom's side of the family. I ended up doing the blood draw, but then passed on the testing as it cost close to $1,000.00. That would have been an out-of-pocket cost to us, and the results were usually less than five percent coming back as an actually genetic-related cancer.

We came home not very impressed or comfortable with these doctors doing the surgery. We had asked the nurse if we could get different doctors, but were told they couldn't break up the team. We had been praying for God to open doors and shut them as He saw fit, so we would know the direction to go. We decided to wait on the surgery. We didn't totally dismiss it, but were going to seek other options. Neither of us had any peace going this route at the time.

The following week on September fifteenth, I had an appointment with a naturopath to see what other options I had. She was a positive, upbeat person, and a believer. She was quite encouraging, considering the doctors we had met. She found out through her testing that my liver was not doing too well, and I was struggling with vitamin deficiencies. We needed to get my liver healthy again. I found out through this process that your liver is tied to your immune system. When your liver is not healthy, your immune system is struggling. Your body needs a healthy immune system to fight disease. A few weeks after doing this protocol, people started commenting that my color was looking better. I didn't know I looked that bad before, but when it was a gradual thing I was the last to notice.

During these weeks, I was doing research to see how I could heal my cancer naturally. I was given two DVD sets from two different friends called *The Truth About Cancer*. In them, I learned a lot and started applying different things I was learning. I also learned there were many ways to heal cancer and that doctors across the nation and around the world are treating cancer without doing surgery, radiation, and chemotherapy. The surgery could cause the cancer cells that were not contained in the tumor to move as soon as the body was opened up. Cancer does not like oxygen, and the cancer cells would move as soon as they came in contact with oxygen. Radiation could cause cancer. I would have had four weeks of radiation. The drug Tamoxifen, which I would have been on for a minimum of five years, has serious side effects and could cause cancer to show up in other areas of the body. Also the survival rates to the five year mark with these procedures have an average of 2.1-percent. Ninety-seven percent of people who have chemotherapy die within five years and also damage the DNA, which could lead to cancer. Usually a person will have another form of cancer show up during their lifetime. As I found out all this, I was determined to heal naturally despite what my doctors told me. Most people don't die from cancer; they die from the side effects and the treatments done on the body for the cancer.

As my body started detoxing from the supplements and herbs I was on from my naturopath, my energy level was a roller coaster ride. Some days I would have lots of energy, and then there would be days where I just lay on the couch with no energy whatsoever. At times I wondered if I would ever have my energy back. A friend, who had gone through a similar experience, said that I would once again have my energy back, and I needed to go through this process to heal my body.

A few months into this process, I had an appointment to see a holistic dentist about the gold crown I still had in my mouth. It had bothered me off and on over the years, pretty much since the dentist had put it in. I went in, and the dentist did some tests to see if the tooth was still alive and also took an e-ray of the jawbone where the problem tooth was. The e-ray showed infection sitting there in the jawbone, and the tooth was no longer alive. I then had to decide whether to have her pull it out or go to an oral surgeon. It was a decision I alone had to make. I was not very good at making decisions at this time because I was so tired, and making decisions was too hard. I decided to have her pull it so I could have the ozone therapy done, which promotes quicker healing. She pulled the tooth out and also removed the ligament in the cavity. This is normally not done in the dentist world, but holistic dentists realize the importance of removing the ligaments so as not to cause infection build up in the bone later on. When she pulled out the tooth, there was a large clump of infection attached to the top of the tooth. The dentist was tearing up a bit because she understands what infection in the jawbone can do to your body.

I asked to see the tooth meridian chart. A meridian chart shows how each tooth is tied to different organs in your body just like your spine, hands and feet have different points where they are tied to different organs and places of your body. The tooth she had just pulled has a meridian tied directly to my left breast. Exactly where the cancer was! This was one of the pieces I had been searching for—what had caused my cancer.

Pulling this tooth released many more toxins in my body. I worked with my naturopath to get the infection and mercury out of my body. This took quite a number of weeks and many days with very little energy. Thankfully I had the great support team of my husband and children who were able to cover everything when I could not.

On my low energy days, I did a lot of reading and research and praying about how I got my cancer. I had changed my diet and ate organically 80% of the time. Diet plays a big part in overall health; especially with any disease, including cancer. I now had added juicing and limited my grains to only sprouted grains or sourdough. I also quit using all sugar, including natural sugar, and used only stevia and xylitol for sweeteners. I didn't use much dairy anyway, but really limited it even more. These are the three things to avoid to shrink your cancer—grains, dairy and sugar. These add dampness to your body, and the grains and dairy turn to sugar, which feeds the cancer. This causes inflammation in the body, so you need to dry out the body.

The biggest area of having good health is the digestive system, which is the immune system. If you are having digestive issues then you are having problems with your immune system. This is where I was having problems. I had been picking up various bacterial infections throughout the last five years or so, but because of the infection of my tooth, this compromised my digestive system more and more.

Emotions also play into the digestive system. If you have any emotional trauma in your life, it will affect your digestive system. This is where we carry our emotions. In the fall of 2015, we had been going through an adoption process through the state foster care system. We were asked to adopt four little children. We had talked about it as a family, prayed about it, and knew we were at peace about going ahead with the process. We all knew these were "our" children. They were in the transferring process and were in our home every weekend from October until December. I had started getting sick right before we were told we were not getting the children because of all the stress involved with the children's social workers the last few months. Grieving for the four little children who were no longer ours was one of the hardest things our family has had to go through. This greatly affected me, and this began a four-month process of picking up bacterial infections and working through all the emotions involved with losing the children.

In February, I had gone to the doctor for a physical, and I did not have any lumps at all. August was when the lump showed up. Because of the emotional loss, my body could no longer fight and allowed the tumor to grow fast. Since my digestive system was already weakened from the dead tooth, and was continuing to fail, my body was ripe for the cancer to grow. Going through the grief process was the final straw for my immune system to fight.

Through all of this, I have learned a lot about how the body works, and through research and prayer, God has shown me how to help heal my body. There is so much research and information out there if you want to heal naturally. You have to be willing to find the resources and people to help you find alternative methods. There are many who have gone before and blazed the trail to cure cancer naturally. I am now in the biggest challenge of my life to do this naturally and heal my body completely from cancer.

Remember that God is good all the time, and all the time God is good! ▇

LYN SCHNEIDERMANN *is the wife to her wonderful husband of over thirty years and mother to four wonderful adult children. She attended Northwestern College in Minnesota and transferred to Minneapolis Business College where she graduated with a diploma in accounting. She then worked in the corporate world but came home to be a full time mom. She home-schooled all of her children from birth to graduation. She is currently assisting her husband in their second-generation family business doing the books and whatever else is required when you own your own business.*

Lyn enjoys spending time with her husband and children and going on travel adventures together. She also enjoys reading, researching healthy living, cooking, sewing and scrapbooking.

CONTACT INFORMATION
Lyn Schneidermann
kevandlyn86@gmail.com
Phone 320-333-7675

10

Grace Bubble

Brenda Sell

In a matter of fifteen months, my whole life changed. I became a widow after forty-one years of marriage, the primary caregiver for my dad who also passed, my mother who was my business administrator became critically ill and was moved to a nursing home, my pet dogs died, and I was diagnosed with an aggressive form of breast cancer and started treatment. For a while, it seemed like my nightmare circumstances would never end. It was tough, but there's an old saying: "When the going gets tough, the tough get going." The key is you just can't give up! Peace remained my close friend—a peace that comes supernaturally. I call it the "The Grace Bubble."

I've been reflecting back to determine what pulled me through in order to help YOU go THROUGH YOUR nightmare circumstances.

What Do You See?

One key is to see. You morph into the picture of the way you see yourself in the situation. I remember the first time that I was referred to as a widow. I read it in the paper. It hit me like a ton of bricks—a widow! What did that mean? What does that look like? How does that change me? How does that change things around me? I didn't know anyone close to me who was a widow so I had no role model. When I heard that term all I could think of was black, dark, depressed. But I knew that wasn't me. As I began to plan the funeral service, my first thought was: *If you're the widow, sit on the front row, wear black, say nothing, and mourn.* Then, I began to re-evaluate what was best for me, what would be best for the people, what would honor my husband. I decided that nobody, *and I mean nobody,* would be able to speak, inspire, and encourage people to live their lives to the fullest through His eyes better than me. I knew that by inspiring others, inspiration and encouragement would come back to me. I had to change the way I saw myself so I could go through this with peace and purpose.

Are You Willing to Fight?

Honestly, when I was diagnosed with breast cancer my first reaction was to not have treatment. As I was praying, I sensed the Lord asked me to consider two questions: Do you want to live? Has your purpose been fulfilled? Fair enough questions. I spent almost a week seriously contemplating these two questions. My conclusions were: *Yes! I want to live and No, my life purpose is not fulfilled.* The next step? FIGHT! When I made the decision to fight, I knew my focus would be my faith. Faith sees beyond your circumstances and has a focus on the outcome—going through the process. I never saw myself as a victim or gave into feeling sorry for myself. I made a decision to see myself well, to do the things I knew were important in order to come out of this and protect my faith. I didn't even tell very many people in the beginning.

Choose Inner Circle Friends Wisely

I didn't want sympathy. What I needed was empathy. There's a difference, you know. Sympathy says, "I totally understand and agree with you, so I'll join you in the pity party." Empathy says, "I totally understand where you are coming from, but have you considered this option...." In other words, sympathy agrees with you and keeps you on the same destructive track, whereas empathy understands but focuses on helping you find a viable solution. One of the most important decisions we make on a daily basis is who we bring into our inner circle of friends. Do these friends feed our faith, or do they feed our fears? This is a critical question that needs to be answered, especially in hard times.

Giving Up Is Not an Option

Do what you know to do, and avoid what you know not to do. Some things you know instinctively, others by experience, and still others by direction from the professionals. I know the value of exercise and was determined to stay as active as I could during the process of both grief and treatment of breast cancer. In the hospital, I would walk 6-8 laps several times a day whether I felt like it or not. At times, my body didn't want to do it, BUT I knew it was good for me so giving into my body was NOT an option. Discipline is not always easy, but it will carry you through. Giving up is not an option when you know there is a fight. The only fight I had was the fight of faith. What did I believe? What would be the outcome if I didn't do what I knew I should do? Because I had already settled the question of fighting, now it was simply a matter of following through with my decision. *You* can do the same thing.

You see, I went through a lot. My life before all of this was a "princess" life. A good family, love for God, no sickness, good health, great business. Then…a barrage of nightmare circumstances. The foundation for success was faith in God and the character that was built in the good times. I never had fear. I always had peace. Yes, I had pain and discomfort, but I also had peace in the midst of it all. One day, as I was thanking God for His hand of protection and peace in my life, I realized I was in the Grace Bubble—a place of total protection from the outside circumstances penetrating into my spirit. A place of total peace that comes from trust and a relationship with God through His son, Jesus Christ. What's even more amazing? The Grace Bubble is available to you, too! ■

Grandmaster Sell releases weekly inspirational videos
to help encourage others. Sign up today for your weekly
dose of encouragement at: Tkd.GrandmasterBrendaSell.com

GRANDMASTER BRENDA J. SELL.

Life is full of challenges. Brenda Sell is no stranger to challenges. She is a pioneer of women in Taekwondo. She has climbed the ladder of success by achieving several world titles including the world's highest-ranked female in Taekwondo Chung Do Kwan. She has forged her way to the top in a male-dominated sport.

Her late husband, Sr. Grandmaster Edward B. Sell, was declared a Living Legend in Taekwondo. He carried the title of the highest-ranked non-Korean since 1964. He was her husband of 41 years, her best friend, and her teacher. Together, they held the title of the Highest-ranked couple in Taekwondo world-wide.

The Black Belt Character Traits of focus, discipline, courtesy, faith, confidence, integrity, perseverance, self-control and indomitable spirit were put to the test when her husband was diagnosed with acute leukemia. Nine months later, he passed from this life to the next. In addition, during the next 24 months she would face the death of her father, a critical illness of her mother, a major change of staffing in her business, the death of her pet dog Princess, and her diagnosis and treatment of breast cancer.

Hope, encouragement, and peace are words that others use to describe her part of the journey. She will share how YOU can go THROUGH your nightmare circumstances. The secret is to go through—not give up, quit, hide, or shut down.

This chapter can help you make it THROUGH YOUR nightmare circumstances and still keep your sanity while looking forward to the future.

CONTACT INFORMATION
GrandmasterBrendaSell@uscdka.com
facebook.com/GrandmasterBrendaSell
P.O. Box 1474
Lakeland, FL 33802
863-858-9427

11

I Teach! – What Is Your Superpower?

Manu Shahi

When the song *Someone Who Believes in You* came out and had the lines "So when you're searching for that rainbow I will help you find it, and when a mountain stands before you I will help you climb it," a picture was painted for me of a superhero. Not in a cape or a fancy car, but an ordinary person who touches someone's life to make it extraordinary.

We humans often want to be shown the big picture. However, it is not always in our best interest as we can quickly become overwhelmed. At that moment in time, the superhero walks in and puts that one piece of the puzzle into your game of life, and it becomes a game changer for you. If someone had told you when you were a child about all the jobs and all the relationships you would experience, along with each one's inherent ups and downs, you would have become overwhelmed. With your head full of information about the future, you would have had a very hard time experiencing your life in the present moment, which is where everything happens. In many ways, we see, hear, and experience things as life unfolds, one chapter at a time, which helps us grow. To help us grow, we often have a difference maker as a guiding light, in person or in thoughts, walking next to us.

While signing the paperwork for selling my franchise, a quiet remark made by a franchise branch manager made me get in touch with my inner self and ask myself to validate what he had just said. He said, "Losing you is a big loss for our franchise and the students because you have been a difference maker." It was at that point I remembered the song and wondered if I ever wore an invisible cape. Even though I was following my passion, the roots went deep, and the branches were spread to give shade to others. It was at that moment I recalled what Zig Ziglar often said, "You are designed for accomplishment, engineered for success, and endowed with the seeds of greatness."

This seed was planted in the summer of 1988. Trusting your inner wisdom may be awkward at first, particularly if you grew up around people who taught you to look to others for answers. I had just received admission into my junior year of school in India. I had completed the paperwork to graduate with a Bachelor of Arts degree. At that stage of my life, I had been raised in an environment of being a self-learner, with no coach. I was one of those students who never crossed paths with teachers and never got noticed either. I don't recall any moments where I was validated by a teacher. I was equipped with everything one needs to be successful, but I had neither a push from anyone at home or school, nor an internal drive. Then the moment came for me when my superhero arrived, leaving a lasting impression and a memory that planted the seed in me, forging my future.

Since I had enrolled in college with no career path in mind, I had no goal nor any dream for my future. I was planning to be busy, but not necessarily productive. Until that moment when I was called to the teacher's lounge by my English teacher, Ms. Bakshi. She was sitting with another English teacher, Mrs. Dhamija. They both looked at me. Then Mrs. Bakshi looked right into my eyes, and without exchanging any greeting, her first sentence to me was "I don't see that you have signed up for the honors program. What's wrong with you, Manu? Are you going to graduate with just a Bachelor of Arts degree?" A tall lady with an unyielding personality, and without giving me a chance to utter a word, she signed me up for the English AP class and planted the seed in me that sprouted into a tree that is still helping to shape me into what I am today. She was my Superhero and my first Difference Maker because she saw something in me. What she did not know was that her courage to change the tide in me, to nurture me, based on who she thought I could be, took me out my comfort zone. The strength that I got from her started to peel open the shell I was living in and helped the real me begin emerging.

A difference maker is an ordinary human being who knows his passion and dreams, mixes it up with experience, and is not hindered by egocentrism. They are the ones who add 'extra' to the ordinary and get their energy by serving others. If we just take our time and look around in our life, we meet such people daily, but we seldom take the time to acknowledge them. How many parents ever realize that they give their children, the most precious thing in their lives, to a teacher for 180 days a year, eight hours a day, five days a week? Relationships made with a teacher last a lifetime. We might not be in touch, but we know how they touched our lives. The child looks at them with an invisible cape, a magic wand, or perhaps wings that will help them fly. They try so hard to impress the teacher every day.

I remember in 2004 my daughter started her schooling as a homebound student in kindergarten. Due to a medical problem, she was unable to attend kindergarten on campus for an entire year. The school district decided to do homebound schooling.

Kindergarten, as we all know, is a significant chapter for parents and perhaps, in its way, a huge moment for children when they feel like a grown-up in a body of a five-year-old. Hearing all her friends talk about school—the cafeteria and how the school looks inside, the drop off and pick up, and recess—made Janvi sad in her heart and eyes. She would often ask me what school looked like, and I would take her to an empty school where she could run around on the playground. But it was not the same.

It was the morning of the 100th day of school when her homebound teacher called to say that today, instead of her, someone else would be coming in to be with Janvi. We were surprised to see her kindergarten classroom teacher, and she brought with her a CD that gave Janvi a virtual tour of her school. The video took her to different rooms in the school showing her what a typical day looked like and ending with the entire class asking Janvi to come back to school soon. That gesture and extra step taken made a five-year-old feel special and a part of the class. It gave Janvi a boost of confidence. That is what Ms. Maxwell from Forest Vista Elementary school did for her. Ms. Maxwell became a difference maker without the cape (but a boot on her foot—she had some issue with her ankle) who made me learn so much as an educator. These two teachers became my starting point.

It was in 2007 that I decided to step into the education industry by opening a math and reading coaching center. In ten years as an instructor, I have crossed paths with just under 2,000 students. When my branch manager mentioned that comment to me I question myself. How many of them remember me as a difference maker? What did I do to become one? Was I even close to the first teacher who believed in me and made me graduate with honors?

A teacher is the weather of the classroom, whose mood makes the difference. As a teacher, I realized that every day I carried the power to make it into a sunny day or a tornado. My words could make a child's life miserable or joyful. I made it my personal responsibility that every student would leave my center feeling challenged and a bit smarter. I was responsible for so many of them, and I could feel the responsibility inside me. Every single day when I walked through the center doors, I knew the challenge and responsibility lie with me, as the parents had trusted me with their kids.

With time, I had adopted this mantra and passed it on to my staff: each teacher has the superpower to change the way the school feels and looks. A teacher, a coach, or a guru—however we want to address them— have been a part of our lives. The tremendous power that a teacher holds by welcoming the students to the classroom with a handshake, look of encouragement, or words of confidence can make the school look like Disney World to the child. Okay, not exactly Disney, but an Adventureland for sure. This power does not end in elementary school years but becomes more empowering as we move forward in life as students. A teacher is not a motivational *speaker* but a motivational *teacher*. If she is a speaker, she will just make you feel good. But if she is a teacher, she will make you feel good, and the next day you will know *why* you feel good, too. She would know that motivation does not last long, as Zig said, but neither does taking a bath. That is why it is recommended daily.

In my teaching journey, I crossed paths with a beautiful Hispanic girl, Samantha, who was adopted by her aunt. Her mother had left her at birth, and her father was unable to take care of her. While her aunt paid for the classes, Samantha lived with her grandparents. I would often see her left behind when the rest of the family would take mini vacations, but she never complained and was content, as she was grateful for having a home. During the three years she was my student, she always had the same smile. Unfortunately, due to personal circumstances, Samantha's aunt wanted to end her classes as she was unable to afford the program—a pre-teen alone with her aging grandparents who at the time were both fighting cancer. I saw her smile disappear and her work ethic going down, and she had lost interest in her studies.

I decided to take her under my wing and paid for her tutoring in return for her promise to perform. My staff and my family became her family, and soon her smile was back and so was her confidence. But once again, due to a medical emergency, she had to quit the program, and I lost touch with her. Three years later, I received a letter from her, and I can say that after reading that letter, my eyes, my soul, and my heart were trying to find Samantha for I wanted to hug her. Today, I know she is okay and is in AP classes and making all A's in high school, and that faith I had in her gave her the wings that made her fly in life.

Every hug I received at my center gave me more power and the charge I needed to keep going. Every time a student would ask if they could talk to me privately in my office, it gave me the confidence to keep going. Every tissue that I handled and every tear I wiped off gave me the courage to hold on as more needed to be done. My communication style with the students was becoming incredibly powerful and efficient. When a student failed a test, it was fear of parents that made them more nervous than failing the test.

My talk with them was never about the failure, but about another chance to master what they missed so they would not have a hard time later. When a student is struggling or has setbacks, don't focus on their abilities. Focus on what they can learn from it. Working with a diverse ethnic group of students, I learned cultures have very different beliefs about effort and ability, and by asking subtly different questions, you can get different answers.

Failure in sports might be important to one ethnic background versus failure in math to another. As a teacher, it became challenging at times to carefully phrase the words so the child continued to perform. On the flip side, I did gather that being entitled was a mindset that kids carried whenever they walked into the classroom. The attitude of gratitude was decreasing. At times, taking the learn-from-failure message too far actually backfired, too.

If they were being told that"you can learn anything and you've done everything you can and you're not getting anywhere," then maybe at a certain point they stopped trusting me as a teacher. I had to develop open lines of communication with parents, but there was a very difficult, fine line between parents and me, helping children enough so that they can do things on their own that they couldn't do otherwise but not helping them so much that they expect other people to do it for them and don't get pulled up to a higher level.

"You slowly pull back as the kids get better on their own, but not let them flail around so much that they get frustrated and give up."

Teaching them the difference between *quitting* and *stopping* was important to me. I told my students that they could leave anytime, but if they stopped before they had met their goal, it would make them see themselves in a different way. It is a teacher's role to equip the child with the goal-setting method that helps him/her with what they are learning. I was not teaching kids for the next day but equipping them to be tomorrow's good citizens. The only person they were competing with was themselves. The parents in my community started saying that at my center I made it hard for kids to quit. I know I did because I was busy developing young difference makers for our society.

Confident young learners were working every day to develop and empower themselves with confidence and academic ability to make a difference in their own lives and that of others around them. I was not raising them to pass the grade but to have the confidence to live life. Many a times I would find students cheating from the answer book and just copying the answer. When confronted, it was denied. But as a teacher, I decided to change the fear of a teacher, the reason a child lies, or has a breakdown. I made it a learning opportunity for both. I would pull out the same worksheet and make them redo the work. It would either show my skill as a teacher for underestimating the student's ability or misunderstanding my own. It would teach them for once it is okay to step it up and take responsibility. Either way, learning was happening.

My teaching method was now taking the shape of a philosophy that I learned as I experienced the joy of teaching every day. It was not where I was teaching but how I was teaching. For me, being the owner of a private tutoring center called Kumon, I totally believed in its founder's philosophy. He said that every child has potential. It was the instructor's role as a teacher to find the potential in the child and show it to them so that they built up their confidence and started achieving things on their own. Thus, we could develop confident self-learners. In almost a decade as a business owner and an instructor, I have seen the wave of change coming toward the method of learning. As someone once said, "Don't limit your child to your learning for he was born in a different time."

It does not make a difference if it was Toru Kumon in Japan, or Rabindranath Tagore in India, or Nelson Mandela. The message is the same—education is important, and every child will learn. Maybe not the same way and maybe not the same day. The truth is, there are horses throughout the world that have the potential to run 1,000 miles, and surely, these are amazing horses. However, though there are many great horses, it is rare to find a person with the skills to develop them. There are also many children of excellent ability. They are everywhere. But there are very few instructors, coaches, or teachers who can discover their potential. Any child, or at least most children, should be able to advance much further than they do in life. The teacher is the difference maker. One of the challenges was a shift in parental style.

Today's generation has shifted the method of learning. These are different times when children are being raised by parents who have changed the parenting paradigm to that of this new era. The dinner table has an Apple device not fruit, paper books don't kindle the desire to read, and emojis are easier to type than emotions to express.

Thus, I had to shift my teaching paradigm based on the new era, but keep the foundation the same. I never stopped believing in the child. But finding the WHY behind a good or a bad behavior was a very important learning method I had adopted. It became very important to me as a teacher to find the WHY behind the performance, both good and bad.

There was one incident at my center when a fifth grader didn't complete her homework on a consistent basis. When asked why, she told my staff that it was hard for her. At the same time, her mother came to me, furious that her daughter refused to do her work because she told her mom it was too easy for her. I was confused with a contradictory answer, so I asked my student why there was a discrepancy in her reply. I called the mother into my office and told my student to express why she had not been completing her work.

At that moment, I was expecting the level of math difficulty to be the reason, but she took me by surprise when she told her mother that she was afraid of her and her screaming. Mother's loud voice and her fear made her be dishonest with her mother. I was proud that the girl got to voice her opinion, but sad that a mother, by changing her tone, could have expressed her parenting concerns much better. She was too busy *correcting*, and not *connecting* with her daughter. Since that day, besides working on her math skills, mother and daughter started to work on their relationship, too. A teacher is just not in a classroom alone. She goes home with the child in some form, too.

Making a difference as a teacher does not mean giving up what you are doing or being earthshaking. You don't need a teaching certification to be a teacher. There is a teacher, a substitute teacher, a coach, a tutor, a trainer everywhere. Are we not all teachers to our kids? And our kids are our teachers too, teaching us lessons of life at every new step or decision we make. Taking an hour a week to coach your child's baseball team or going to a local school district and being a mentor to the at-risk kid, helping a new employee at work to get better—you're teaching.

It is hard to make a difference if you have eyes only for yourself. You must take the focus away from yourself and shift it toward others. A huge difference can be made when you decide to help in the area you are already good at and know the rules. You become an indirect authority and earn respect because you know what you are doing.

Most children should be able to advance much further than they do in life. Children can progress, but often have no one to help them. If teachers believe that children can't advance very far, children won't have the chance to progress. The positive energy passed on from a teacher to a student in the form of a note, verbal acknowledgment, or a high five are energizing notes for a student. But on the flip side, a harsh word, remark, or action can also impact a student for life. It can turn the tide the other way.

It was in the winter of 2014 that I had a chance to go back to India for my twenty-fifth school reunion. There were more than fifty of us who made it from all over the world to celebrate what our school gave us as kids. It was during the three-day retreat when we all realized how the education system has evolved over time, and back then the traditional classroom style of teaching the top 1% made us feel left out. But irrespective of what school offered us, most of us had someone who believed in us.

One of my school friends, a beautiful lady, poised and elegant, shared her story with us. A successful executive in a pharmaceutical company in Atlanta now, while in school she was told by one of her teachers that she would amount to nothing. As a school kid, you end up believing either your parents or your teachers for everything. Life gave her a chance to spread her wings by letting her do what she loved and learn what she loved. With that, she improved her academic standing. At every milestone, the teacher's voice used to resonate in her head and push her to move forward.

And then one day in 2000, while visiting India again, she saw the teacher standing and waiting for a train to arrive. At that point in her life, the executive had completed her Ph.D., received an NIH and a NASA grant, and was completing a postdoctoral fellowship at the Cleveland Clinic. The teacher's harsh voice rang in her ears as she looked at her teacher—old and tired. Was that due to age, or words? Even though my friend wanted to go up to her teacher and say something. At that point, my friend was stepping into a new life and the teacher had stepped down, so maybe for a moment they were even. The only difference was life made one a teacher by profession and the other by character. My friend told herself the voice that once pushed her was just noise, and it was time to tune it out. Now she held the controls.

No child or adult wants to feel irrelevant. No matter how small their dreams are, they want to make a difference—stepping out of the box, risking their reputation and getting up to do something different. Every person has the same number of seconds in an hour. How we use those seconds leads to something more meaningful that makes a difference. It was my passion for the kids to see themselves succeed, finding the WHY for their behavior, understanding their teenage behavior, and connecting the parents with a child that made me step outside of my comfort zone. I learned that we all love to stay in our comfort zone in life. It is only when we step outside that zone that we enter the learning zone. Learning perhaps from the students, new teaching methods, more styles, new technology, etc. But the circle after that is where we get scared—the Panic Zone. We fear failure. We are afraid of judgment, and that makes us run back to our comfort zone. But once we are in that new zone where we have learned new things and overcome any anxiety or panic, we enter the END ZONE—and we have scored a TOUCHDOWN!! We become a difference maker in our own lives. Those around us learn from us, and at that moment, we plant a seed of greatness in their lives. The same seed that was planted in mine by my teacher.

I left my comfort zone in 2015 and stepped into the learning zone. I got certified as a motivational teacher and started doing workshops for teens on self-image and goal setting along with running a center, but then I realized that my WHY as a teacher was bigger. I needed to connect the dots—parents with the child. Every conference I had was more about parenting than academics, about messy rooms when I saw messy relationships, about time spent on gadgets rather than being together. I could see more than I could absorb. Hence, I decided to step outside the learning zone, and I stepped into my panic zone. As a woman, leaving a comfort zone was hard, but I decided to sell my business and start a new journey. I decided to move to a new zone as a teacher and become an academic life coach where the need to coach those who are stressed about grades and going to college was important. To help today's youth to find the WHY and help them spread their wings. As I sit and write this chapter, I also write a new chapter of my life because in this chapter I plan to take kids, parents, hopes, dreams and wishes that we make it to the end zone. A new zone where all children are equipped for success and ready to handle their lives ahead. To make them aware that deep inside, one day they all will dare to be difference makers.

MANU SHAHI *is a graduate of the University of Texas at Arlington, who bid adieu to the corporate world and entered the education world in 2007. She became a certified instructor to coach students in math and reading. She realized that kids and their families lacked proper goals and guidance on relationships. She became a Ziglar Certified Trainer with Zig Ziglar Corporation. She did not stop there when she realized that there was a gap between what students were learning in schools and what was useful in life. Many of the skills required to be successful in adult life—such as leadership, communication, core motivation styles, and academic thinking styles—are simply not directly taught in schools. She also realized that many students struggle with stress about grades, frustration in relationships, and anxiety about college, and that is when she discovered Academic Life Coaching.*

Manu's love for learning and passion to help made her add to her skills by getting certified as an Academic Life Coach.

Her mission is to connect with families and partner up as a coach for teens through a consulting program which naturally help students develop the skills that are useful in high school and college. She also works with women through her coaching program, Women Who Win—helping them with everyday work-life balance issues.

Manu Shahi is actively involved with the Make-A-Wish foundation and the Lean In.org as a moderator, empowering kids and women for a better tomorrow.

She lives in Flower Mound, Texas with her husband, Sandeep, and daughter, Janvi.

CONTACT INFORMATION
Manu Shahi
Speaker/Academic Coach/ Consultant
info@manushahi.com
www.manushahi.com
972.333.4663

12

The Journey to Financial Freedom

Eric Shelly

If you are like most people, you spend a great deal of your time creating the income you need to support your family and your lifestyle. If you are lucky, you do something that you love to earn that income. However, if you don't work, there is no income. As you read about the experiences of the contributors to this book, you'll notice the theme freedom has many facets. From the time we begin our career until the day we retire, we are striving for financial freedom. In the infancy of our career, we are seeking freedom from debts, from student loans, or maybe business startup expenses. Maybe you bought a home, and your eventual goal is to be free from the mortgage. You are excited about your new career, and you realize that you can trade your time and energy for the income you need to support your lifestyle and, of course, your debts.

After a while, you realize that your time is also a facet of your freedom. You feel the pull of many things that demand your time including your career, your family, and your need for personal time. As you begin to pay down your debts and start to build up assets, you realize that through investments, you can create passive income streams. Passive income can create the freedom that you want by displacing the need to work for active income. As your passive income grows, you have the freedom to take more time off work. You can also use your passive income to accelerate your accumulation of assets to create an ever-increasing stream of passive income.

The ultimate freedom comes when your passive income allows you to do whatever you desire. You may choose to travel, play golf, volunteer, or even work. Whatever you decide to do, if you have adequate passive income, it's your choice. That is ultimate freedom.

The stories in this book will show you how the theme of freedom played out for each of the contributors. In these stories, you are likely to find parallels to your own situation. Each of my colleagues is in a different place in the pursuit of freedom. Most of us have taken different paths, but the common theme of all of the other authors is that they all took action, in some cases, massive action.

I encourage those reading this book to take your first action. It will lead to the momentum you need to begin your journey to freedom. There are many options for getting started. Most of the contributors in this book partnered with a knowledgeable real estate investor in their first deal. Partnering gives you the opportunity to learn with the protection of someone who has knowledge and experience in doing that type of deal. You will benefit from the experienced investor and will gain access to appropriate deals that you may not otherwise have access to.

Congratulations to those of you who decided to take action. You are one step closer to freedom. Your momentum will build, deal after deal, until you finally achieve your goal of financial freedom. We hope that your journey to financial freedom is as enjoyable for you as it has been for us. What follows is the story of my journey through dental practice and on to financial freedom.

My Journey to Freedom

Two years after I graduated from dental school in 1991, my wife (also a dentist) and I bought our first dental practice from a doctor who was retiring. The deal included the purchase of a building that had a dental office on the first floor and apartments on the second and third floors. When we took over the practice, my wife and I moved into the second floor apartment and leased out the third floor apartment to a tenant. We had just graduated from dental school with over $175,000 in combined student debt, and we had just borrowed another $60,000 from my mother-in-law for the down payment on the practice and the building. We financed the practice through a local bank and paid $60,000 for the practice and $280,000 for the building. Like so many other 26-year-old doctors, we found ourselves over a half million dollars in debt before seeing our first patient.

I was still working as an associate in another dental practice when we took over the practice. This practice had limited space, making it difficult for my wife and me to treat patients at the same time. In 1996, we established a startup satellite practice in a nearby town, which gave me the opportunity to leave my associate position. We negotiated a lease with the landlord for a space that was previously leased to another dentist. We then leased the necessary equipment to outfit the office and one operatory. Both offices continued to grow over the next couple of years. We managed to always pay all the bills, but there was very little left for savings. Whenever we seemed to be making enough money for any savings, we would end up owing significant taxes, and that would bring us back to reality.

In 2000, we finally outgrew our original building and sought out a larger building to house our growing practice. The building we bought was eventually renovated to expand our office space to nine operatories. With the growth in both practices, it was now necessary for us to hire an associate who began working in the satellite practice. We continued to struggle to save money because we were spending so much on growing the practice. From adding equipment to hiring additional employees, we couldn't get ahead.

We finally sought out a financial consultant to evaluate our situation. The major revelation from the consultant was a suggested restructuring and refinancing of all of our debt. By consolidating many equipment leases and refinancing the building at a lower interest rate, we were able to lower our monthly debt payments by $8,000 a month. From that point on, we have been able to follow a wealth accumulation plan that has led to our financial freedom.

Eventually, we realized that the practices were becoming very different in nature. The original practice was expanding its procedure mix and becoming very technology oriented while the satellite practice remained a traditional restorative practice. Faced with the high cost of outfitting both offices with high-tech equipment, we decided to sell the second practice in 2007. With little or no startup investment other than extending our credit line approximately $30,000, we managed to increase our original investment by a factor of 10. This was the first significant amount of capital that we ever had to invest. We also realized that focusing our energy on the original practice increased its productivity, and growth skyrocketed.

Within six months, we decided to hire an associate dentist who would eventually become a partner two years later. The practice buy-in created a second windfall of capital for us, almost three times the amount as the first practice sale. By the time we did this transaction, I had figured out that I was actually harvesting equity from my practice as my career was progressing. This is very different to what many dentists do. Typically, they practice their whole career by themselves and then try to sell the practice at the end of their career. I wish I could say that it was a clever strategy that I came up with, but I was really just reacting to the situation as it evolved. The trade-off for working with a partner is that you can sell your practice for much more than it would be worth at the end of your career if you sell pieces of it during its peak value.

With the capital from the practice sales, I was able to begin investing and creating the nest egg that I needed to retire. At the time, I was still putting most of my investments in the stock market. However, I began to feel uncomfortable with my investments in such a volatile stock market. I began to look for diversity in my investments. I began looking at alternative investments such as commodity trading, real estate, and other business ventures. I was fortunate to find a group of like-minded professionals in an organization known as Freedom Founders headed by Dr. David Phelps. This group is made up of dentists, veterinarians, doctors, and a group of trusted advisors in various segments of the real estate arena. The symbiotic nature of the group gave me the confidence to invest in real estate in a much safer fashion then I would have otherwise. With access to the real estate deals that are available within this group and the education I received from this group of trusted advisors, I was able to invest the capital which I had accumulated over the years into real estate investments that have created passive income for me. The amount of passive income I was able to create through my real estate investments was enough for my wife to be able to retire. Imagine what it was like to give your wife the freedom to retire and to pursue the passion that she has for horseback riding.

In discussing my wife's departure from the practice, my partner and I also explored the possibility of buying out the balance of the practice at an earlier date than we had originally anticipated. We both analyzed our individual situations and determined that selling the practice at this time was actually in both our interests. Although I wanted to continue to practice, I was more than willing to give up control of the day-to-day management of the practice in order to pursue my real estate ventures while at the same time continuing to practice for approximately thirty hours a week. The sale was actually completed early in 2016. At the time I am writing this book, my monthly investment income has been in excess of my previous dental income for the past three months, and there are still several passive income streams that have not yet started. I still feel a great passion for dentistry, and I am nowhere near ready to give up taking care of my patients. There is a definite sense of freedom when you are practicing for the sheer joy of practice as opposed to practicing with the pressures of meeting overhead and making payroll. To finally take a vacation and know that your practice and your income will not suffer because of your absence is incredible.

My Journey with Real Estate

My involvement with real estate started when I was a young boy. My father and my uncle began investing in apartment buildings when I was very young. They went to a local banker who loaned them money to purchase a house. Then they renovated and divided that house into two or three apartment units. I can still remember as a young child hanging out with my dad and scraping off layers of old wallpaper because it was one of the few jobs that I could do. I wasn't old enough to swing a hammer or carry a two-by-four, but I was proud to be working with my dad. Over the years, my father and my uncle ended up owning approximately eight buildings with 15 rental units.

I believe the equity in the building was one of the big things that allowed the bank to finance that practice for us. Had there not been a building along with that I think the bank would've been very hesitant to loan the money to a couple that had just graduated from dental school and had over $150,000 worth of debt. We had become accidental landlords who really didn't know what they were doing. More by luck than intention, the revenue from the apartment and the rent we were saving by living and working in the building was enough to cover the mortgage on the building. Managing the apartments was easy because we were working and living in the building.

Eventually, we purchased a larger building for our practice. We considered keeping the first building as an investment property, but we really didn't have the money to renovate the first floor and carry both mortgages. We also found that managing the property without being on site all the time was more challenging. This is a lesson I would soon forget.

After practicing in the new office space for several years, we had saved enough money to begin investing. My next adventure in real estate involved buying a rental property in a partnership with a friend of mine who is a broker for Edward Jones. We decided to buy the property off of the retail market so we ended up talking to a real estate agent who was a good friend of ours. We bought a duplex in our hometown, which had a student rental permit. Our town has discontinued issuing student rental permits so this was actually a bonus. We ended up paying a retail price. The property needed minimal renovation and was very easy to rent. We had very minimal vacancy over the five years we held it. But I had forgotten that it was much easier to manage a rental property from on site. The other thing that I learned from this particular adventure in real estate is that it's very important to buy rental properties at a wholesale price—about 70% of market value—in order to achieve a good cash flow. Ideally, you want to buy properties after all improvements have been made, and that way you are able to manage cash flow properly.

After selling that rental property, I was becoming disenchanted with the stress of owning and managing rental property. I put most of my investment dollars into stocks and bonds. Over the last three years, I saw that the performance of my investments were very lackluster. With the returns I was getting, I would need an extraordinary amount of savings to retire as planned. Frustrated with my portfolio, I started looking for other options. I started investigating Freedom Founders Mastermind group because it was made up of many dentists like me, and their focus was safe investing in real estate using joint ventures with real estate experts. I decided to "dip my toe in the water" to see if this was a good fit for me so I signed up for my first meeting and was pleasantly surprised.

My first joint venture deal was a hard money-lending note where I supplied the funds to purchase a wholesale property and to renovate it. Once the property was flipped and sold, the investor paid off my loan with interest and points all in about ten months. The ROI in this investment was at least three times greater than I was accustomed to. I was serving as the bank so I was protected by a mortgage, a promissory note, and I was named as an insured on the property insurance. I did a little research on the property and the area to make sure the numbers were accurate, and I used Google Earth to view the property and the surrounding neighborhood. I also spoke to at least three other investors who had done deals with this investor. To know I was dealing with someone who knew the local market and who had expertise in appraisals, I felt very safe with the investment. Since then I have done over thirty-five short term hard money loans and have invested in a fund that pools capital to do similar loans. For a busy professional, these deals require very little effort once you have completed your upfront due diligence.

My second joint venture deal involved the purchase of a turnkey rental property using traditional 20% down financing at 4.75% interest. I chose a three bedroom, two bath single family house that was at the upper end of the affordable housing spectrum for about $140,000. I used a turnkey rental company that finds properties that can be purchased and rented so that there is a reasonable cash flow. The advantage to using such a company is that they have contacts with mortgage providers and property managers that have been vetted. Everything is in place including the tenant. If I had to find all this support on my own, I would probably invest in less rental property.

It is still important to do the same type of due diligence to assess the value of the property, to evaluate the neighborhood, and to interview the property manager. Once in place, turnkey rental properties provide a monthly passive income that shows up month after month. What a great feeling to passively collect a steady stream of monthly checks from your mailbox! Turnkey properties have more management issues than lending deals. You will have tenant issues such as late payments, repair requests, vacancies, and placement fees. These issues are handled well by a good property manager, but you have to allow for these unexpected costs. Higher risk but higher potential rewards.

Of course, I didn't stop there. I continued to buy turnkey rental properties. As you move forward, you will want to consider diversifying your rental portfolio. You can diversify by buying in different regional markets. The likelihood of all of your diversified areas suffering a downturn in difficult market conditions is reduced. You can diversify with price points. You can also invest in different types of property such as apartments, single-family residences, multiplexes, new construction, or renovation. I felt comfortable with new construction 4-plexes because there would be fewer repairs, and I was able to put four doors under a single mortgage.

I also like the single-family houses with rent-to-own tenants. I have invested in five different geographic regions to create some diversification. As of this writing, I have created a substantial passive income with a diverse portfolio of twenty-eight rental units.

So as you can see, it is possible to parlay your working income into assets that will provide you with passive income. With action and persistence, you will eventually create enough passive income to cover all your expenses, and you will experience the joy of financial freedom. It is my hope that you will be inspired by my journey through professional practice and the real estate investment arena, and that you too will find yourself on your own path to financial freedom.

DOCTOR ERIC SHELLY *is a gener-
al practice dentist and real estate investor who grew
up in Lancaster County, Pennsylvania. After earning
a Bachelor of Arts Degree in physics from Franklin
and Marshall College in 1985, Dr. Shelly graduated from University of Pennsylvania School of Dental
Medicine in 1989 with a Doctor of Dental Medicine
degree. He immediately began private practice as an
associate in two practices before acquiring his own
practice from a retiring dentist. Practicing with his wife, Dr. Margaret Lee, Dr.
Shelly continued to grow this practice and created a second startup practice in
1996. He sold the startup practice in 2008 and added a younger partner in the
primary practice later the same year. In 2016, Dr. Shelly and Dr. Lee sold the
practice to their partner. Dr. Shelly continues to practice approximately thirty
hours a week as an associate in his former practice.*

*As a real estate investor, Dr. Shelly has created a portfolio of twenty-eight
rental properties, five funds controlling over 425 doors, and has funded over
thirty short-term hard money loans. He is a member of the Freedom Founders
Mastermind, and he serves as a mentor to his dental colleagues in achieving financial freedom. Dr. Shelly has started an annual business symposium
through the Pennsylvania Academy to help dentists with business practices
and personal financial management. He is also working with individuals who
are interested in safely participating in joint real estate ventures.*

*Throughout his career Dr. Shelly has been active in community service
and has served as a leader in organized dentistry. He has been the president
of his homeowner association and a longtime member of the Exchange Club of
West Chester where he served as the newsletter editor, board member, treasur-
er, and president. He has hosted a free dentistry event called PAGD Cares for
the past eight years that provides free dental care for over 100 patients every
year. He was the local chair for the Nation of Smiles event at the Philadelphia
National Convention of The Academy of General Dentistry. Over 350 patients
were treated in this one-day event by over eighty volunteer dentists. Dr. Shelly*

also volunteers at the Community Volunteers in Medicine Dental Clinic on a monthly basis.

As a leader in the dental profession, Dr. Shelly has served as a board member, vice president, president-elect, president, and immediate past president of the Dental Society of Chester and Delaware County. He went on to serve as a board member at the Second District of the Pennsylvania Dental Association.

Dr. Shelly is also a member of the Academy of General Dentistry, an organization of 40,000 general dentists, where he is currently serving as a trustee on the national board. At the state level, he has previously served as a board member, continuing education chair, vice president, president-elect, president, and immediate past president. His passion is clinical dentistry and helping his colleagues achieve success in their practices and in their financial security.

CONTACT INFORMATION
ericshelly@verizon.net

13

Unusual Paths
The Women Who Influence My Journey

Sheila Steinmark

My journey has taken me down paths that most women don't travel, but each step of the way, there have been people who have taught me and encouraged me to take the next step. Each path and influencer led me to the next path; together they have inspired, and taught me along my Journey.

My Earliest Path

My first lesson was of silent empathy, spirituality, a sense of belonging from an unlikely place…right next door. Growing up in a suburb of St. Louis, I was a pom-pom girl, in drama club, a member of the student counsel. People thought I had everything. I did…which included a secret of abuse. Mrs. Commuso, an elderly widow, somehow saw through the façade and reached me to my core. She started with simple gestures of kindness and friendship, and then invited me to join her at church. While she never discussed what was happening at home, I always felt she knew. Sunday afternoons upon returning from church, she would light a fire in her fireplace and prepare lunch for us. Most of the time, before she came back with our sandwiches, I would be asleep in front of the fire. This ritual continued off and on for years, until I left home.

Then, an Unexpected Path Change

My parents had just gone through a divorce and unbeknownst to my mother, I was left with my abuser. I was a week away from attending the University of New York to study International Business with the hopes of then going to Law School, when my father moved to New York for the purpose that I live at home while attending school. I left early the following morning after the most difficult confrontation of my life. After a cross-country trip back to St. Louis, I enlisted in the U.S. Army as a Legal Specialist.

My Military Path

I spent the next six years learning and growing. I spent time with the 101st Airborne Division, 2nd Infantry Division (Korea) and back to the 101st where I deployed to Saudi Arabia and Iraq in Operation Desert Shield and Desert Storm. As a legal specialist, I spent a lot of time supporting the Criminal Law Division, which for me was therapeutic.

During my time in combat, I learned about leadership, strength, courage, and friendship. I had served with an amazing group of women; we referred to ourselves as the PMS Brigade. Our fearless leader was Master Sergeant Kathy O'Dell. She was career Army and as tough and driven as any man I had ever met. She was a calm, steady force, and when needed, she would give you a swift kick in the butt. Until the battle started, boredom and home sickness were our biggest challenges.

The battle started and ended within days. I spent my 23rd birthday in Iraq with a gas mask on and a rifle across my arm. I heard artillery fired from behind me and watched the flares land in front of me. The second they touched the horizon, the mortars started exploding. All the while, Kathy kept us focused and motivated, but on occasion added a bit of humor, reminding us that if the generals had let the PMS Brigade go in months ago, we would already be on our way home.

The flight home from Iraq was just like the Budweiser commercial. We had a layover in New York. As I deplaned, I felt my hand being squeezed. I looked up into the eyes of a Vietnam-era soldier who had come home to hatred and protests. I saw the crying eyes of my Sergeant Major. His hands were shaking, and he looked as if he would be physically ill. I remember his sobs when we entered the airport to deafening applause and screams of a cheering crowd.

My New Career Path

After six years of active duty, I joined the Illinois National Guard as a part-time soldier and full-time student. After bouncing around a bit, I landed the job of a lifetime at the in-house marketing agency at Anheuser-Busch.

In September of 1995, I joined Busch Creative Services, as an administrative manager. In the eleven years, I spent there, I was promoted four times and eventually, I left as the Director of the largest mobile marketing fleet in the nation. I thought I had learned about the Boy's Club in the Army. It paled in comparison to working at a brewery, managing a fleet of Mobile Marketing Vehicles. With the guidance and championing of a handful of people to whom I will forever be grateful, it was the ride of my life.

My first promotion was to Associate Project Manager. I worked for a woman who taught me how to champion for other women and fight the glass ceiling. My first day in my position, all the background materials on my project, The Mobile Beer School, came up missing. A Technical Director threw a business card at me and told me to "spec my own F'ing generator," and I found out that the guy who tried to feel me up at the Christmas party was part of the 16-man team that reported to me. I had champions that I never expected, all of whom I was grateful to, but Tracy Garrity not only championed me to three promotions but helped me double my pay in the nine months I worked for her. She also gave me an acronym that became my rally cry. I had been called "Bitch" so many times that it became … Boys I'll Take Charge Here! That rally cry took me from a $2.5 million program to managing a $21 million department.

The Path to Enlightenment

In May of 2000, I learned about unconditional love. While I always had received it—I hadn't understood it. I had taken my mother for granted, not understanding all she had given of herself and the lengths she would go for me...until I held my newborn-daughter, Sammi.

My mother had been a victim as much as I had. She is a scrapper and refused to fail, but she has the kindest heart. Many of her friends refer to her as St. Joyce. While I was deployed, I received a letter every day, and she rallied her co-workers into adopting my unit. Every soldier, from my Commander to the newest private, received care packages every month and every holiday. If she did that for strangers, you can imagine how she treated her children and granddaughters. Her love I had taken for granted, but quiet nights as a single parent, alone with my daughter, allowed me to reflect upon her unconditional love.

While I built my marketing "creds" and raised my daughter, taking a class here and there, I served as the Chief Legal Non-Commissioned Officer for the Illinois National Guard. I became the Senior Instructor at the Military Academy, later the Operations Sergeant of a Chemical Battalion and retired as the First Sergeant of a Chemical Company.

During those fourteen years, I learned to be a leader. I found my passion for public speaking, and I met a woman who inspired me so much that her seeking and cherishing my friendship and counsel gave me a confidence I never knew. We traveled countless miles visiting Guard Units. We would get so engrossed in conversation that we would go miles only to back track because we had lost track of where we were. I was often a guest in her home and grew fond of spending time with her and her family. I was in awe of her strength and wisdom, while a loving parent and giving friend. I know her as my dear friend and mentor, Alicia. The world knows her as General Alicia Tate-Nadeau, the first general in the history of the Illinois National Guard.

As I have followed many paths, I have made so many friends. As a single parent, I learned the value and necessity of the Community of

Women I call my girlfriends. From my sister-in-law, Barbie, who kept my daughter when I needed to travel, to my work friends that became my life line, there are so many cherished friends that regardless of how much time passes they are simply a phone call away.

I lived in the same condo complex as Christina and Suzanne, my co-workers, neighbors, partners-in-crime, and best friends. These ladies and their teenagers played Santa, took care of my daughter when I was sick, picked her up from school when I was running late, and became our extended family. When Sammi and I had moved to the Boston area, my daughter was on a flight to St. Louis when the airport was hit by a tornado. Sammi's flight got diverted to Chicago. Lindsey, Christina's daughter, was there before Sammi's flight landed and treated her to an adventure until her father could retrieve her.

There have been just as many amazing men in my life as women: my step-dad who became the dad I needed, my twin brother, supervisors, co-workers and friends, most of all, my husband and best friend, Jim. However, it is the lessons I've learned from the women in my life that were the inspiration for so much in my life.

My Next Career Path

After moving my daughter and me to the East Coast for my next career path, I found myself as the Vice President of an experiential marketing company that allowed me to work with a small, scrappy team that accomplished cutting edge programs that turned the marketing world on end. I worked on programs that are now taught in college marketing classes.

I was new to the area, alone with my daughter and knew no one! What was I thinking! I had been told that New Englanders were stand-offish, cold, and hard to get to know. None of that was true. These ladies I barely knew came to my rescue and rallied around Sammi and me. Not only were they the friends and confidantes I needed, they were my back-ups for my daughter's care, and they vetted the man I was to marry and share my life with.

A New Turn

Five years after moving to the Boston area, my path took another turn. I married the love of my life and three weeks later, we packed up and moved to a suburb of Dallas. Jim had been relocated by his employer, Perot Systems, which shortly after became a division of Dell. It was the catalyst for my next adventure.

For the first year in Dallas, I worked at the agency remotely. It daily became more of a struggle until it forced me into action. In June of 2012, I found my first client and started my own marketing agency. I spent the first year traveling non-stop. I landed a consulting client, a national tour, and was hired by my previous agency to complete programs I had been an integral part in producing.

When the projects were finished, I finally came up for air and realized two things. First, the guy I hired to bring in business hadn't delivered so I didn't have any work. Second, I didn't have any girlfriends in my new home. My husband and daughter had made friends, and they went to work and school each day. I was now home all day and felt alone. I had met people. I just hadn't built the types of relationships I had in the past, and I missed them.

My Most Rewarding Path So Far

This realization led me down my next path. Between growing a business and creating an infrastructure of people I could count on, I was led to one of my most difficult but rewarding paths. It took courage I never knew I had. I called eight women I had met and invited them to join me for a glass of wine and the opportunity to make some new friends. That night I found my voice and my purpose. I invited women at different stages of their careers and lives.

We talked for hours that night! From the beginning, I knew it wasn't a typical networking group. By the end of the evening, I found the courage to tell the ladies what was happening with my business. As soon as I said it, I felt that it wasn't as insurmountable as it had felt. Through their encouragement and counsel, I had my head together again. I was up for the challenges of my business. While my paths aren't always easy, I will continue to face challenges and succeed.

Looking back to that night, when I shared my business concerns, I think I shocked them with my honesty. We each opened up and talked about what we needed from one another. It felt empowering. From that night on, we have grown to a group of women, 91 strong. Our group is comprised of a corporate CEO, a top-rated financial advisor, several ladies in the oil business, a nurse, a pharmacist, others who founded non-profits, small business owners, direct marketers, authors and speakers, those employed for small to large companies, teachers, retirees, and stay at home mom's looking to get into the work force again. Each of the ladies offers something different and is so valuable. The strength in a group is our differences and the desire to keep learning from each other.

I have felt empowered and inspired, sharing my experiences and knowledge and learning from these ladies. I am a mentor to them, as they are to me. I was looking for trusted friends. What surprises me is that they look at me as the leader and mentor. As I benefit and learn from them, I am sure I get more than I give.

My Journey continues and as paths show themselves, I know that I'm not on this Journey alone. There are and will be more amazing women to lead and follow. ■

SHEILA RONDEAU STEINMARK,

Owner, Marketing Operations Group, LLC

As a marketing operations leader and innovator, Sheila has produced complex and highly recognized marketing initiatives from development through implementation. Having spent 20 years in the agency arena, she has positioned her clients as global leaders by driving sales with creative and operational teams by building key relationships that support corporate goals.

Sheila possesses a unique skill set in operations, logistics, leadership and problem solving. Her combination of operational and management skills has allowed her to repurpose them to drive large-scale mobile marketing, product sampling, social media, pop-up retail, trade show and brand building that exceed business objectives.

Before starting Marketing Operations Group, Sheila worked for several marketing companies, including the in-house marketing agency of Anheuser-Busch where she ran the largest mobile marketing program in the nation. She has worked on programs such as: Budweiser Mobile Beer Schools, Budweiser True Music Roadhouse, Glaceau Tasting Vehicles, UPS Centennial Celebration, Anheuser-Busch National Sales Meeting and Expo, P&G's Tide Loads of Hope and Mile of Style, Charmin NYC Restrooms, Kellogg's Pop-Tarts American Idol Sponsorship and Pop-Tarts World, Sony Youth Sports, Corona Beach, and Turner National Bracket Day.

Another aspect of Sheila's career has been her military service. Sheila is a retired Army First Sergeant and a combat veteran from the 1st Gulf War. Sheila served for 20 years from 1985 until her retirement in 2005, which included active duty for six years with the 101st Airborne Division, Ft. Campbell, KY, and 2nd Infantry Division, Camp Casey, Korea, and an additional 14 years in the Illinois Army National Guard.

Sheila grew up in St. Louis. She currently lives in Dallas and is blessed to share her life with her supportive husband Jim and 16-year-old daughter Sammi.

To check out case studies and more, please see Sheila's LinkedIn Profile.

CONTACT INFORMATION
Marketingopsgroup.com
Sheila@marketingopsgroup.com
214-856-5816

14

Where Did I Go?

Mary Stryker

Have you had those moments where you looked in the mirror and wondered who is looking back? The image you see has some wrinkles, a few gray hairs and what is that thing under the chin? You just look and think *Really??!! Where has the time gone? I don't feel nearly as old as I look!*

Now, some of you reading this may not be at that stage yet. Sorry to inform you, your day will come!

Time flies when you are having fun. It certainly has for me. Even with the new aches and pains that show up uninvited on a daily basis, I still see myself as a youthful 30-something that is just enjoying life. I do my best to avoid mirrors. I like the 30 year old image much better!

At this point, you have figured out I have been around for a while and hope to continue this journey for many years to come. So, to the question of where did I go, a little background of where I have been.

Where Have I Been?

I was lucky to grow up when I did in a loving family, nothing but good memories. I was a typical kid, but I was a bit of a loner with an independent streak. It was also not the era of a jam packed schedule with sporting events, etc. Most time was spent running around the neighborhood. I had a few activities that kept my mom on the run: dance lessons,

I had a pony, that kind of thing. Sports were done in school, and being competitive wasn't me.

As far as school went, it was just part of the daily routine, but being the loner that I was, I wasn't involved in much besides going to class. No class president or homecoming queen on my resume. The grades were okay, but nothing came naturally. I don't recall my parents being too worried that I wasn't a straight A student.

Seems I could always find something else to do besides study. I believe I would be considered ADHD if I were going to school in this day and age. The word "test" sends chills up my spine.

I had a bit of an attitude and temper as a child. If I didn't get what I wanted, be prepared for a lot of whining, pouting, etc. It seemed to work. There are some good stories about the lengths my parents went to get me what I wanted just to shut me up! I also did not like to be told what to do. I outgrew the temper issue but not the being told what to do. Was that a sign of early confidence or just being a brat?

So, fast forward to college. What a whole new world—new friends with such interesting backgrounds, interests, talents, and outlooks on life. I was in a sorority which gave me the opportunity to spread my wings a bit. How fun it was to be a part of such a vibrant community!

I don't remember any conversations while growing up about having dreams, self-esteem, self-confidence, setting goals, having a why. All that was not a big topic of conversation but as I look back, so many of my friends were a lot braver and had a confidence I seemed to have lacked. You couldn't have told me that back then.

How Did I Fit In?

I was so excited that I had found a place that I "fit in," where I may not have been the star athlete or top student my friends were, but I was always there to cheer them on, whether at a sporting event, if they were a talented musician, singer, artist, were running for some office, etc. I was their cheerleader. In return, I was surprised by how much others saw in me that I was not aware of. They had a way of making you feel like you were good at anything and everything. That your being there mattered.

I ended up in this particular sorority thanks to an invite to a "sister's weekend" from a family friend who didn't have a sister so she invited me. At one point in the weekend, they did a little "Soul Train" dance line. I fell in love with this group at that moment. We watched Soul Train at home (showing my age here) and my mom, brother and I would be "doing the line." Dad just watched. So when the music started, so much for the quiet loner, I was right in the middle of the fun with everyone cheering me on. At that moment, I knew I had found a group I wanted to be associated with.

I was thrilled to be asked to be a member, and the next four years (yes, you could do it in four years back then) was filled with learning, growing, cheering on my friends, and of course dancing!

Knock me over with a feather when I was asked if I would consider the office of president of the sorority. Well, if they thought I could do it, why not! Talk about a self-esteem booster, which at that point I was not sure what that meant or that I needed it!

Before I knew it, it was graduation time. I had a diploma. It was time to get on with life, which I had no real plan for. I just figured that work and family were on the horizon so off I went looking forward to the next step in life.

The Real World

Out of school and into the real world. I moved back to my hometown of Kansas City, got a job and an apartment with some college buddies. Life was good. That independent side of me was a happy camper.

Then life got better. I met this really incredible guy. His beautiful curly hair caught my attention first. A mutual friend (who I didn't know I knew but he knew me) introduced us. He was a dental student. We had gone to the same college, lived close by but ran in very different circles so had never met. Besides being really cute, he had me laughing at his first comment. I was hooked. The amazing thing was he was, too. Funny thing that I would be surprised that this really cool guy wanted to spend his life with me! But, yay for me, and off we went with a bright future ahead.

So, fast forward 30+ years through twelve years with the Army which we loved. It also included orthodontic training. That has been followed by the start up, growing and running of a very successful orthodontic practice.

We loved the army, but due to changes in the dependent insurance set up, it was time to go out on our own. We ended up in a small rural community where we knew no one, started a practice from scratch, and then waited for someone to walk through the door!

I had had various jobs while we were with the military and at the time was enjoying being the WIC nurse at the health clinic in our community. An odd job for someone with no kids, but I liked it. Well, a new business needs help. I was excited to jump in, but working with your spouse can be tricky. Hey, it has worked for us thanks to laying out a few guidelines. The one thing I was sure of was there could only be one boss, and that wasn't going to be me! I wanted the team to know who was running the show, so to speak. I had witnessed other couples working together, and it seemed they were always butting heads about something. Since I wasn't an orthodontist, I let him take the lead, and he has pretty much figured the rest out with some help from me, the cheerleader. (Sound familiar?)

The practice has kept us busy to say the least. I have been a part of it all on a daily basis, holding many positions, but my most important roll has been cheerleader. (There is that term again!) Your team may be wonderful, but it can get very lonely and frustrating being the only guy in a bunch of women.

It is truly amazing, humbling, and a bit scary to see where we are in comparison to where we started.

Making It Work

To keep up with running any business, continuing education is an important aspect of staying on top of things and making sure you have your life in order so you can keep your business in order. Part of running a business, and life in general, is to never stop learning, and read, read, read!

My really smart, cute husband was way ahead on this, always reading both dental and motivational information, and all things in between. The key is that he has an incredible power of concentration, actually absorbs the information, sticks with it until he understands it then actually puts it into practice.

On a road trip to visit family many years ago, he popped in a Zig Ziglar CD, or maybe it was a tape. It was so long ago. It was good stuff, but at this point in life, it was all about the business. All the info about goals, vision, being productive, sharing, and helping others seemed to pertain more to how we ran the practice. But, Zig made an impact, and self improvement was now on my radar.

The passion of always working to improve yourself has been something encouraged in our practice. We have an office library filled with all the books my husband has read. (I am way behind in the reading department). You would think that just looking at the person he is and how he leads his life thanks to all this knowledge he gets from reading (add podcasts to that list) would be an inspiration to jump in and start reading/learning! I try to keep up, but that independent/ADHD streak takes over.

I also may want to read something else that is just for entertainment. There is a bit of a guilt factor there. I know my reading choices could be more impactful, but at the same time, the books I was reading drew me in. I was immediately connected to the characters and the story. It was sad when I finished the book. I now realize that maybe this loner is a bit lonely, and those books fill a void.

So Where Am I Now?

I am in my early 60s, and hopefully there are many years ahead. Now is a big time of change. Selling the practice is the big one. That has defined us for years. We have been changing lives for years, giving people of all ages the smile they have always wanted which in turn gave them more confidence to go do what they dreamed of doing. We want to find a way to continue to impact lives.

There is also the huge concern of making sure that financially we can continue to live the life we enjoy while at the same time be giving to impacting others. What do we do next, and how do we do it?

We have gotten some good guidance on this, but most of it has been about how the doctor finds a new path, one that gives purpose to life. It is suggested you think of something you have always loved doing that lights a fire in you, what you are passionate about. Build a business around this activity that allows you to do what you want, when you want, with whom you want. Have a why attached to what you want to do. Good advice and my husband is so excited to get the ball rolling. He is a builder and problem solver, and this is right up his alley.

After listening to all this information at one particular meeting, all the sudden it hit me, WHAT ABOUT ME? My life is taking a turn, too. Wow! Where did that come from?

I have been worried about my husband stepping away from something that he feels defined who he is. I was thrilled to see the new fire in his eyes. The cheerleader was right there, but something else clicked in.

What about me and my future? Wow again!

I was reminded of a doctor at a meeting talking about his wife who had had the dream of buying the little shop she had been working at. That didn't work out and the doctor was struggling to help her find something else to do. Maybe have her work in his office? That comment has stuck with me. Something tells me that job at the shop was a big part of her identity beyond being the doctor's wife and a mother. Having the shop for herself was not only her dream, but there was probably a desire to just have something of her own. I know the doctor was just trying to find something to help fill the void for his wife. I just hope he realized how much was behind her dream of having the shop.

So what about that thought that popped into my head? It was an ah-ha moment. It was the beginning of looking back at where I have been, where I am now, and wondering about what I want the future to hold. I also realized that even though I am so proud of who WE are (my husband and I), I have lost a bit of who I am.

There are several things I would love to change when I look in the mirror, but I am averse to needles, knives and, "being put to sleep." The rest of the story … I can't change it and wouldn't if I could. But there are some questions to be asked and lessons to be learned.

Why have I always been the cheerleader? What made me gravitate in that direction? I love that role, but what kept me from being the brave one, doing something big and bold?

So, I was never the best student or a gifted athlete. (This would be considered negative talk these days.) I assume my life would be different if I had thought that my self-esteem was low, and I needed to work on my confidence. But somehow I survived, and as mentioned before, life has been good.

As I look back and remember some of the things I used to really enjoy, I realize that somewhere along the way I stopped doing them. What made me quit? Did I just get lazy? Am I depressed? Did I think I should be doing something more valuable with my time?

Back to that ah ha moment. I don't know why at that particular time a light bulb went off. I even remember being a little mad. It was all about the doctor which was no surprise since this group is based around doctors and other professionals. Since that moment, I recognize the importance of a dream and some clarity of things I may have been missing and wanting to make up for some lost time.

As you can surmise, if asked what I am passionate about, I would not have a quick answer. The question of what has brought you joy and lights a fire in you is easier to look back and find.

So Where Did I Go?

I have been to some amazing places. There are probably many who would love to have been in my shoes, not much drama or tragedy, lots of love, family and friends, security. Where do I go now, how do I get there, and how do I make it better than where I have been?

Age brings wisdom and the chance to learn and have guidance. (If you will just take it!) I think on this next phase I want to turn that cheerleader roll more to myself. It will be a challenge for someone who is a bit set in her ways.

I can see where I want to be and what changes I would need to make to get there. That is the first step, a vision. I certainly have some work to do to get some balance and motivation in my life which I am sure will give me more confidence to build on the ah ha moment of "what about me?" With that vision and some cheerleading from others I see my husband and I both fulfilling some dreams we didn't realize we had.

Not long after that ah ha moment, I started doing one of those things I used to do that I really enjoyed but for some reason quit doing—antiquing. Talk about lighting a fire! There is one little shop I love. The owner and I can talk for hours. She has such pretty things and has such a talent for displaying them. After one of my lengthy visits to her shop, I left knowing I wanted a shop of my own just like hers. Another ah ha moment!

My husband was certainly surprised when I announced what I had in mind. Here we are trying to get away from a business! We are working on a plan for a business that can be run from anywhere with virtual employees, if necessary. After the shock wore off, I think he was excited to see me excited about something! I did promise I would not drag him to too many antique stores or make him do a lot of heavy lifting. So any volunteers to help with that?

This idea is going to take some research and planning to make it work with some of the other plans we have for our future. I have mentioned it to a few people, and the response I get is "that would be so perfect for you" or "you have to do it, that is so cool!"

This is in the early stages, lots to consider. No doubt there will be work involved. Just the thought of giving people the experience of being surrounded by such pretty, fun things, having people come into my shop and get the same joy I have when I go into my friends shop. That will be so awesome!

Having this dream/goal has been motivating. That independent side is kicking in in a good way! I don't plan to give up the cheerleader role. I just need to remember to cheer myself on!

It would be interesting to know why I chose the cheerleader role and stuck with it all these years. It really doesn't matter. Life has been good and I look forward to the future being even better, if that is even possible.

So are you wondering who that person is looking back at you from the mirror and wondering where the time has gone and the "old you" went? I hope like me you see that where you have been has been good, but the future can be better. May you have an ah ha moment that lights a spark that leads to places you didn't know you could go.

MARY STRYKER *is a native Kansan, but not by much. She grew up in Kansas City on the Kansas side but on State Line Road. Just walk across the street, and you would be in Missouri.*

Mary and her husband, Ross, are both Kansas State graduates. Someday they plan to move back to Manhattan, Kansas, home of K-State, where they can enjoy the beautiful prairie and participate in all the activities a college town offers. Especially the football games—

Go Cats!

Mary is married to an incredible guy, and they have shared thirty-four years together. Along with Mary's help and a top-notch team, her husband has run an awesome orthodontic practice. Being the only orthodontist in a three county area, can you say busy? It has been humbling to be a part of changing lives. There is no end to what a beautiful smile can do.

What gives Mary and her husband the most joy are their dogs. Cairn Terriers (Toto dogs) have been in their family for over 30 years. Mary wasn't sure about this dog thing all those years ago when her husband expressed the desire to have a dog. She hadn't had a dog growing up. So, Mary got to pick the breed and to this day feels that was one of the best decisions she ever made, next to saying yes to marrying her husband!

Magic got it started. It took one second to have Mary's heart stolen by this precious animal. Magic was followed by sisters, Snickers and Twinkie, and now two more sisters, Munchkin and Ozzie. What lessons they've taught us. The joy for life they have is infectious and so entertaining—not to mention the love they give. Their house is truly not a home without a dog(s).

Their love for dogs prompted the start of PAWS, Pet Awareness and Welfare Support. This organization helps with finances when an animal is in need of health care that the owner cannot afford.

The future looks bright for Mary, her husband, and furry buddies. Who knows what lies ahead, but if it is as good as what has already been, then how lucky and blessed can anyone be?

CONTACT INFORMATION
mary@strykersmiles.com

15

The Time is Now!

Amy Thibeault

I have learned from your example that if you work hard and really put your mind to it, you can achieve virtually anything.

~ Mindy Hassell Muellenborn, Flower Mound, TX

Not another minute! Not another hour! Not another day! I remember this day all too clearly as I was sadly looking at myself in the mirror on a cold day in December of 2010. I was incredibly disgusted about the way my body looked and decided to get on the scale for the first time in a few years! WTF…250 pounds! I weighed more than some male black bears! Hogs are usually taken to market when they weigh 250ish pounds! In the 2015 NFL season, of the 1,746 active NFL players, the average weight was 246 pounds. UGH!!! I looked at myself in the mirror and said out loud"I AM DONE!"

I immediately went to my closet to look for shorts, shirts, socks and athletic shoes because I had just found some serious inspiration to move my ass! I pulled out my 2X yoga pants, my XXL t-shirts, and my athletic shoes from high school. Next, I walked to the computer to start googling upcoming races in the area. Not just any race for this girl! It would need to be a full marathon, whatever that means! I had to Google it! Twenty-six point two miles, 46,112 yards or 138,336 feet of running. What could possibly go wrong? I hear of people completing them all the time, and most people don't die. I totally can do this! I will lose some weight. I will check it off as a splendiferous thing to do, and I will show my family how cool I am! Oh, and I will get a new t-shirt! I ran and found my husband to tell him the good news, and being the amazing guy that he was, he was instantly supportive! I am sure he thought I was insane but he never said it out loud. I registered for the Fort Worth Marathon to be held on November 13, 2011. The website said "fastest, flat Boston Qualifier in North Texas," and almost everyone loved the race because it was easy to get a PR. What the hell is a PR? I'm so thankful for Google! I thought this was the perfect race for me because it would be fast, flat, and maybe it would prepare me to run in Boston one day! I had no idea what I was doing. This is THE DAY that I DECIDED to change my life, but I had no idea how powerful this decision would be. This is the day I became a runner!

The next morning I was out the door at 5 a.m., and I decided I would do my very own training plan that I refer to now as "The Mailbox Training Program." I was going to walk to a mailbox, run to the next mailbox, walk to the next mail box, and so on. I managed to complete a one-mile walk/run/walk that first day, and it was completely dreadful. It sucked more than receiving a gas-powered vacuum cleaner for your anniversary! I had to really assess who I was that day and remember WHY this was a MUST for me! I had a beautiful new daughter, Drey, who was four months old, and I didn't feel like I had the energy to be a great mom to her or my other three wonderful children, Alyssa, Blakelyn and Channing, who were older. I also wanted to be a magnificent, sexy wife more than anything, and over the course of that first mile I found all my WHYs! No more bullshit! No more being a fat ass! No more excuses! This was happening!

You never have to know the HOW when your WHY is as clear as the water in Bora Bora off the French Polynesia. The HOW always comes! Day after day, without fail, I would do the mailbox training program, and over the course of weeks and months, I found myself passionately chasing this goal and truly believing in myself with zero limiting beliefs about completing a marathon. I would take my lunch hours to run in the hundred degree weather! I would wake up at 3:30 a.m. to make sure I was training daily and not missing family time or neglecting work responsibilities. I would run home after my workday because it was exactly seven miles from the office. I persevered on my journey when cars would drive by, and the drivers would say mean things and throw objects at me! By the way, a "shout out" to the mean kids on Briarhill Boulevard in Highland Village, Texas, for all those reprehensible tactics and deplorable comments that you guys made when you would drive by! It definitely intensified my hunger and thirst to succeed, so thank you for that outstanding gift! On a side note, when you see people out exercising, please take the time to encourage them! You do not know their story! Everyone has to start somewhere!

Many people thought I was crazy, and I knew I was! I was crazy in LOVE with the goal of becoming the BEST version of me! Isn't that what we all want? What manifested from this mindset and resolve to complete a marathon was far more incredible than I could have ever dreamed or imagined! You will never regret making a decision to improve your life by stepping up and setting a new standard for yourself. Is it easy? No! Will there be haters? Yes! You never want to regret living an unfulfilled life! Period. This marathon quest taught me several things like how beautiful this world is! During long runs, I would really notice the birds singing, the trees, and the families in parks, the clouds and all of God's amazing creations. My heart was becoming happy! I saw people differently. I started becoming someone I have never known and it felt amazing. I realized that taking care of myself made me a better wife, mother, employee, manager, friend and neighbor. I wanted to give more and contribute more to this amazing planet! I utilized those training runs to dream, practice incantations, and pray. I would visualize success at every level and especially what that would look like crossing the finish line. As my body improved, my mind improved, and I realized who I was and what I was capable of becoming. I had become limitless in my thinking and I had a thirst for greatness in my life.

If you have one takeaway from reading this chapter, I hope this is it: Divorce everything and anything in your life that isn't serving you well! Get rid of people, rituals, habits, addictions, jobs, significant others, and any other nonsensery that is keeping you from being the person you want to become! As Eminem says, "Look, if you had one shot, one opportunity to seize everything you ever wanted—one moment. Would you capture it, or just let it slip? Yo…!" A real decision to change and become more means that those ridiculous bullshit fairy tales about why you are fat, broke, single, unemployed, not happy, uneducated, and scared or whatever are no longer allowed to be played on your playlist! Are you ready to start that business? To write that book? To invest that money? To go on an African safari? To lose weight? To change jobs? To go back to school? To move across the country? To forgive someone? Whatever that "thing" is that you're thinking about right now…NOW is the time! Life is way too short not to become a badass rock star full of life!

I see the finish line about 20 yards ahead! For the love of pickles, I just endured 26.2 miles of exciting, wicked purgatory. Just a few more steps! I can do this! I became a professional deep-digging specialist that day! My thoughts ranged from *I am so happy I didn't die to I cannot believe what a BEAST I am to I can't wait for the next one.* I crossed the finish line in tears because I was not nearly the same person I had been six hours and 53 minutes earlier. As the tears consumed my eyes, I literally felt like the world was mine and I could do anything that I decided to do. I found my strength and courage that day! My life would never be the same. I guess I was right in my initial thinking that running a marathon would be a "cool thing to do!" Six years later, I have completed five full marathons, two ultra-marathons, a 223-mile relay race, and I am the healthiest and happiest that I have ever been! When I stepped on the scale this morning … 130ish pounds! I love the way that one crazy idea coupled with some massive action changed the course of my life forever. The best part…my family REALLY thinks that I'm the coolest mom on the planet!

I have learned to write goals down and work hard towards them. Also, to be fearless about pursuing exactly what you want. I also learned from my amazing friend, Amy, that it's ok to be bat shit crazy sometimes—well, maybe all the time!

~ Candi Comer Fuller, Gainesville, TX

AMY HACKLER THIBEAULT

is a captivating author, motivational mouthpiece, empowerment mastermind, revolutionary thinker, farce comedian, and a transformational scholar. Amy grew up in Gainesville, Texas, and now resides in Aubrey, Texas, with her husband, Joseph Thibeault. Amy is passionate about leaving a compelling legacy for her four children, Alyssa, Blakelyn, Channing and Drey. Amy's life message is to inspire people to live a gratifying and fulfilled life. According to Amy, "Life isn't meant to be lived perfectly but merely to be LIVED—fearlessly, wildly, beautifully, venturesomely, dauntlessly, magically, valiantly and optimistically! And to ALWAYS, always live with laughter and passion!"

Amy Thibeault currently serves as an operations manager for a Primary Residential Mortgage branch in Flower Mound, Texas, and she is the co-founder of the Amy & Joseph Thibeault Foundation. She has two master's degrees, and she serves on the leadership team for the North Texas Firewalkers. Amy enjoys reading, spending quality family time, sending handwritten cards, walking, traveling, attending self-development conferences, organizing events in the community, serving on local boards and volunteering in various walks of life. Amy's bucket list includes having lunch with Tony Robbins, Darren Hardy, Mark Cuban, and Dirk Nowitzki. Amy is working on several projects to be published in the very near future.

"I've had many great mentors, and beautiful humans throughout my journey, education, and my professional career that I would like to thank. A big 'shout out' to the following people: Nancy & Doug Dinnes, Grandma Irene, Norman Gilliland, Jim Mitzel, Lisa-Marie Thompson, Sean Varin, Donna Emmert, Ricardo Leon, Iona Beck, and last, but not least, my parents. You all have impacted my life in a way you cannot even begin to fathom. The role that you've had in my life—regardless of how long or how brief, how positive or negative, how ordinary or extraordinary, has shaped my world for the better.

You have taught me lessons, shown me different paths I could travel, guided me through the ebbs and flows of life, and made an irrevocable impact on who I am now. Thank you!" - Amy Hackler Thibeault

CONTACT INFORMATION
Amy Thibeault, MBA
Cell: 214-907-9334
E-mail: aj@ajtfweb.com
Website: www.ajtfweb.com

16

Braving Infertility Together
A Sisterhood of Hope

Sarah Ivy and Dr. Juli Westcott, DC

One. Pink. Line.

How can everything hinge on one pink line? Experiencing the full grief cycle every 28 days can take its toll on anyone. So you think to yourself, surely getting some answers will help. Knowledge is power, until that knowledge leaves you powerless. You wake up facing possibilities, and go to bed with no hope. In one day, your whole world shifts. The clinical diagnosis of infertility changes more than just how insurance views your medical chart. It changes how you view intimacy, sex, love, your womanhood, and nearly every aspect of your life. From that day forward, you never see yourself, your family, or a crying baby the same again. Things that once challenged your sanity suddenly become the deepest desire of your heart.

Infertility is so much more than failing to conceive or sustain a pregnancy after 12 months of not using contraception. It is the inability to grow your family when and how you want. Words like endometriosis, polycystic ovary syndrome, trouble with ovulation, premature ovarian failure, diminished ovarian reserve, male factor infertility, recurrent miscarriage, tubal factors, and unexplained infertility enter your vocabulary, and you begin to wrestle with the feelings of brokenness, isolation, guilt, and shame.

They say one in eight couples struggles with infertility, and while each family's journey is unique, we share a common goal. When comfort lies in instant gratification, the perpetual "hurry up and wait" of this journey stretches us in ways for which we were never prepared. The weight of infertility can be crushing, and no matter how strong we are, a seemingly unbearable burden. Thankfully, a burden, when shared, is lighter than one carried alone.

> *After going through infertility, you never really think that pregnancy loss, or any type of loss for that matter, is even possible. Then again, I never thought I'd struggle with infertility either. I joined this group five days after my miscarriage. These women pulled me out of a darkness when no one else in my life could. They understood, and I was no longer alone. I struggle with the saying that "everything happens for a reason," but I do believe that God uses our struggles to help and guide us. God led me here, through heartache and unbearable pain, to a place of love, understanding, celebration, and bravery. For that I will be forever grateful.*
>
> ~ K. Newman

The hope that comes from surrounding ourselves with others who have walked before us, and those who are walking alongside us, is invaluable. This sense of community is absolutely essential for anyone attempting to come out on the other side of this in one piece. You no longer have to walk alone, we are braving infertility together. *#bravingIT*

In a traditional search for support instead of community, we find ourselves further isolated. In an effort to protect our feelings, many groups choose to segregate members who are in different stages of their journey. While on the surface, this appears to protect us and validate our bitterness, hurt, and anger, the stark reality is those emotions do not disappear with the appearance of the second pink line.

When my infertility journey started, I began looking for a support group to help me cope with the whirlwind of emotions that occur during this process. I noticed that many online support groups were very "hush hush" about giving support to those struggling with infertility, and finding them in the first place was almost impossible. I found this group just a few days before my FET transfer, and was intrigued by the full range of support that was available. I was discharged from two infertility support groups after I became pregnant, so the support I received from these women has been a lifesaver for me in this part of my journey. No matter what infertility issues the other women in the group are going through, they are willing to set aside those stresses to help a fellow member.

I thank God daily for each member who has become a sister for life.

~ L. Smith

Loving bravely challenges each of us to normalize infertility at any stage in every aspect of our lives. Accepting the truth that we are not alone starts within our own hearts, and changes the way we love and support one another.

In early 2015, this change sparked a movement. With geography as our connection, a small group of women decided to take our friendships from virtual acquaintances to something more intentional. Who would have imagined that a reservation for brunch would become a platform of hope that would change how we face this disease? We are redefining infertility together. *#redefiningIT*

Armed with the mantra of "put your big girl panties on," we are challenged to love beyond the now. Whether you have been recently diagnosed or have struggled for years, have never been pregnant or have suffered loss, are currently pregnant or wanting to add to your family, we meet you where you are. Your path may include timed intercourse, intrauterine insemination (IUI), in vitro fertilization (IVF), donor relationships, embryo or traditional adoption. No matter what, we walk with you where you are. This all-inclusive mindset shatters the lie that pregnancy and infertility cannot coexist.

The love and support I have received from these amazing ladies is immeasurable. We grieve and hope and celebrate together. It's a community built on love where you can share as much or as little as you need. You don't have to explain your struggle in depth because your feelings during this process are completely, intuitively, and empathically understood.

~ M. Young

Infertility can create a space that houses fear, disbelief, doubt, confusion, resentment, envy, and jealousy. It is okay to go to this space, but it is not okay to stay there. We invite you to a safe environment that allows you to be vulnerable and work through your feelings as they arise. We love you where you are. We are embracing infertility together. *#embracingIT*

Battling infertility in a time where we are technology-driven and relationship-starved makes the Internet a necessary evil. Dr. Google can be our worst frenemy as we try to educate ourselves on our diagnosis and up-coming procedures, but at least we know our options.

We even turn to social media in hopes of gaining some experience-based education. These mediums tend to put a rose-colored tint over our lives, causing us to only post our best pictures on our brightest days. This façade of perfection leaves no room for posts about struggle, loss, or grief. Fortunately, our private forum allows us to be completely raw, messy, and honest. Only then can we celebrate together and grieve together. All feelings, thoughts, and questions shared respectfully are welcomed and addressed. With a newsfeed ranging from early diagnosis to alternative treatments, from losses to miracles, we are truly living life together.

Having this group as I walked through one of the toughest times in my life was vital. They knew exactly what I was feeling. They got me. Because so many had gone through it themselves, they were able to love me in a way that only a fellow mother of an angel baby could.

~ A. Sanderson

Our Care Council is in place to ensure that no post goes unanswered, no heart goes unloved, no woman is left alone. Should the need arise, this team's commitment is intentional and personal contact in the first 24-48 hours. The hearts of these women are grounded in integrity, fueled by compassion, and propelled by selflessness. Even in the midst of their own struggles, they choose to set aside personal feelings in order to love beyond themselves.

> *Two years ago, when my husband and I started trying to conceive, I began teetering on a dangerous level of anger with God, as every month my hopes were dashed. As a woman over 35, when I crossed the six-month point, I was heartbroken. Then, as I crossed the year mark, my anger and bitterness really began to manifest. I found myself giving into the depths of depression and hopelessness, and my anger consumed me. Every month the same as the one before, ending with a big fat negative. I began to reach out on my personal Facebook page, not sure what I was hoping to find, when someone I hadn't had contact with in years told me about this group. I can't explain what it's meant to me. It's been my church. It's given me both a vehicle to receive care and an outlet to give to others, and has shown me that giving can be even more healing than receiving. I'm broken over my journey of infertility, but I am grateful that my life is not as broken as it was before infertility. So much of that I owe to the women of this group.*
>
> ~ S. Burris

Our relationships grow deeper through family events where supporters and loved ones can see first-hand the genuine sisterhood that we have cultivated. A unique aspect of our platform is our acknowledgement of our supporters' perspective. It is never easy to watch someone you love hurting. How can they help? What should they say or not say? At designated meetings, we provide supporters a place to share their struggles and gain skills and encouragement as they walk alongside us. Additionally, our annual picnic and regular social events where we open our homes to each other allow another avenue for relationship building.

As our community has grown, we have continued to expand to meet needs as they arise. For those who become pregnant, our Miracle Moms group offers an additional forum for continued support and questions about pregnancy, birth, breastfeeding, and beyond. An added benefit for these women is the opportunity to be a beacon of hope to those still waiting.

> *I've never thought of myself as someone people could look up to. But when I look at the women I've come alongside this year, it makes me feel like I've got purpose. I never thought in a million years that IVF would give me not only a child, but the bonds of friendship and personal growth.*
>
> ~ J. Pierce

All of this pales in comparison to sitting across the table from women who "just get you." At our local monthly meetings, we break bread together and share hugs, tears, and laughter. Finally meeting someone in person whom you have talked to, prayed for, and shared with online is like meeting a long-lost friend. Encouragement, connection, and validation generate authentic conversations and lasting friendships. Our deepest healing is found in these moments. This is the heart of our movement—living infertility together. *#livingIT*

The most common misconception about success in this journey is that at some point, the wound of infertility heals. We have found that even when healing occurs, a scar always remains. Pregnancy, birth, motherhood…these milestones remain clouded by the brokenness, isolation, guilt, and shame we have carried since that first day. This is our new reality after the long awaited, desperately wanted second pink line finally appears. We are forever branded by this shared experience, and while we may never feel like a "normal mom," we will know for certain that we are not alone.

For those still waiting, for those of us who feel like we are drowning in the rain of losses, chemical pregnancies, failed cycles, and the monthly appearance of our period, it sometimes seems impossible to find and hold on to the hope that someday, somehow, it will be "our turn." In the meantime, we find strength in each other, even when life is messy. When faced with pregnancy announcements, baby shower invitations, the panic of a friend who "wasn't even trying," or the well-meaning mother who cannot wait to be a grandma, we have the freedom to vocalize our needs in a safe place. This lessens the sting of ignorance and empowers us to teach others how to love us well. We are overcoming infertility together. *#overcomingIT*

Infertility does not define us. It does not control us. It is a part of us, but it is not who we are. We are not broken. We are not unworthy. We are not worthless. We are brave! With hearts of giants we are braving, redefining, embracing, living, and overcoming infertility TOGETHER.

Will you join us?

BRAVE BOARD OF DIRECTORS

Sarah Ivy,
Founder and Executive Director

When my husband and I got married, we were in our early 30s and began trying to grow our family immediately. Nearly a year into our journey, I was given a diagnosis of Severe Diminished Ovarian Reserve, and my husband, Severe Male Factor, which led to a less than 2% chance to conceive and carry our own biological child. We were lost and felt so alone. This is the time when Braving Infertility Together truly began. We knew that we could love better and could allow others to do the same. We began at a brunch, then an online group, and then these new relationships led us to new options. We adopted two embryos from an amazing family, which resulted in pregnancy...and then miscarriage.

We lost Hannah Joy in July 2015. Shortly after, we adopted seven embryos from another generous couple, and were led to share them with another family. That family welcomed a son, Dawson, in July 2016. While saving money to do a transfer ourselves and celebrating in the joy of those around us, God showed up and showed off! In January 2016, we became pregnant, naturally, and Charlotte was born in September 2016. We are in awe of this little miracle, but are now painfully aware of the guilt and pain of a secondary infertility journey. The Lord was very clear with my husband Ray and I, and led us to sign over the remaining embryos to the other family. This has challenged us to lean on Him to grow our family in whatever way He sees fit. Any time we have followed His call, he has answered our prayers. Ray and I, and the rest of the Leadership Team, are blessed to lead this tribe. Getting to live life with these families is a gift we truly cherish.

Dr. Juli Westcott DC,
Co-founder and Executive Vice President

My first and only natural pregnancy was in January 2004. After two years of trying, it finally worked! Or so I thought...Two weeks later, I had a miscarriage. From that day forward, I never had another positive pregnancy test. Not one. I went through all kinds of testing, but everything came back "normal," and I was told to "just wait" or "keep trying."Through a painful divorce, remarriage, medical challenges, and a cross-country move, I continued to wait and try. Still nothing.

In May 2014, we decided it was time to see a fertility doctor, and were given the diagnosis of "unexplained infertility." Because of my age, after two failed IUI cycles we were told that IVF was going to be our best option. We did our cycle in January of 2015, and, by the grace of God, had a successful transfer in April. A week after finding out I was pregnant, a woman I met through an online infertility group invited me to dinner with her and a few other women who were struggling with infertility. I agreed, but I worried whether they would still accept me if they knew I was pregnant. That is where the distinction lies with this group. They not only accepted me, they welcomed me with open arms. That dinner changed my life, and I believe the lives of many others as well. That was the day that this movement truly began. As friendships grew and other pregnancies were announced, we became a family. We were braving this journey—together.

In December 2015, my husband, Wes, and I were overjoyed to welcome our beautiful daughter, Cadence Joy, into the world. She is our greatest gift, and was absolutely worth every second of my 13-year wait. This journey has been long and painful, but I would not change it or where it has brought me. I am forever blessed by the amazingly brave women who have and continue to walk alongside me.

Rain Stawar,
Chief Financial Officer

I am 40, and have battled infertility officially for three years. I started IVF in May 2014. My first transfer was a success, and I became pregnant with boy/girl twins, Jacob Benjamin and Elizabeth Anne. We felt so fortunate to get pregnant with our first FET, and began preparing to welcome our twins in the summer of 2015. Unfortunately, in February 2015, my parenting journey became a bit more complicated when I went into labor at 19 weeks, five days. While in the hospital, my body became septic, and in order to save my life, we had to deliver the babies at 20 weeks, two days. The proceeding weeks are a blur of tears, confusion and anger. For the first time in my life, I joined an online support group.

One lucky day, I received a message about a local group that met for dinner once a month. I was initially hesitant, but finally went to my first meeting after a few months. At this meeting, I was overwhelmed by the love and support I received from the women in that room. They listened and cried with me like we were sisters instead of strangers who knew each other for less than an hour. This group has helped me find myself again after such a tragic loss. I suspect that I will never fully heal from losing my children, but I am heartened by the amount of love I have for them. This group has supported me through three more unsuccessful transfers, including two chemical pregnancies, and is currently loving me through my husband and I becoming certified as foster parents. This journey has taught me many things, but most importantly, that God is in control. I will listen patiently for His guidance, and know that my Brave sisters are there walking beside me every step of the way.

SARAH IVY *is the Founder and Executive Director of Braving Infertility Together. Sarah has an extensive background in public speaking and curriculum facilitation in the property management field. An active member of her church, Sarah currently serves as a Stephen's Minister.*

DR. JULI WESTCOTT, DC *is the Co-Founder and Executive Vice President of Braving Infertility Together. She is the Director of Health Science Academies for Collin College, and runs and private practice called Natural Advantage Chiropractic. Juli also helps lead worship at her church in English and Spanish, and assists with the Medical Response Team.*

Sarah and Juli met at the group's second "official" meeting, where they shared a time of private prayer. Having both suffered infertility and losses, these women embody a bond that is truly divine. Their passion for loving others in their darkest times is what sparked this movement. Sarah and her husband, Ray, live in Garland, Texas, with their daughter, Charlotte, and two dogs, Lucy and Millie. Juli and her husband, Wes, live in McKinney, Texas, with their daughter Cadence ("Cady") Joy, and their dog, Sheba. Both families are committed to lean on their faith and each other to help carry the burdens of those around them.

CONTACT INFORMATION
Website: http://bravingit.org/
Email: info@bravingIT.org
www.facebook.com/bravinginfertilitytogether/

Braving
Infertility
Together

17

And the Hits Just Keep On Coming...

Wes Westcott

It was 1982. I had just graduated high school. A hard-working, carefree kid with big dreams of playing college football, I was driving a brand new '82 Camero and was dating the Jr. Miss California runner-up. Life was good. Little did I know, everything was about to change...

I was driving up to see my girlfriend, listening to my favorite music, and had all my windows down, the warm summer wind blowing through my hair. I honestly don't even remember what happened, because it happened in the blink of an eye. I woke up in a wrecked car, with my head where the passenger's feet go and my foot tangled up in the steering wheel. When they found me, I am told that I was walking around collecting scattered cassette tapes (I don't remember any of this). The person who found me guided me through the tall bushes up to the highway. Through the ringing in my ears and the taste of blood in my mouth, reality started to set in. I finally put together that I had been in a head-on collision. I was later told that a retired schoolteacher had fallen asleep at the wheel, come across the median, and hit me, causing my car to flip end over end three times and land 60 feet off the road.

Growing up in Carmel, California, one of the most beautiful places in the world, I felt like I grew up in a bubble. I had this security about life. As a high school athlete, I felt invincible. I really didn't have a care in the world, until this happened. When I went to the doctor after my accident, he told me in no uncertain terms that my days of playing football were over. It would be too dangerous for me because of my injuries. My life just stopped right then and there. It was so hard for me to imagine—I couldn't believe what I was hearing. Because of my athlete's mentality, I felt like I could overcome anything, so to be told that I would never play football again was devastating. From that day forward, I started feeling this fear I had never imagined... looking over my shoulder, afraid to drive a car. I was skittish, disappointed, and had pent-up anger. I was like a wild horse stuck in a pen.

I had always been afraid of hurting my back in football, and now here I was, being told that the only way I was going to heal would be to either have surgery on my injured disc or stay home on bed rest. I wasn't interested in either of those options, so instead I decided to see my dad's chiropractor. He worked on me for a couple of months and taught me strengthening exercises for my back. As I began to heal, I was filled with this intestinal fortitude that I was going to be able to get through anything that happened.

A couple of months later, knowing that I no longer had the option to go to college, I just felt like I had to get away. So, I picked up and moved to Colorado. I took a job cooking at a restaurant right next to a ski resort. I would ski every day and cook every night. I continued to do my exercises to help my back heal, which allowed me to be able to ski. I was making just enough money to pay the rent, but in my mind, as long as I had enough money to buy a ski pass for the season, I was happy.

Since I didn't get to go to college to play football, this was my college experience. It was the time of my life. It was the first time I had really been anywhere on my own and met new people. Colorado was a real growing experience for me. It was when I realized that life goes on and there was a big old world out there that I had yet to discover. But as fun as it was, and as nice as it was to be in a resort town and meet so many people, I missed home. Experiencing 33 days of not seeing the sunshine got to me—I missed the California weather. I was only in Colorado for about a year before I decided it was time to "grow up" and go home to start working full-time in my family's construction business.

Several years later, at the age of 27, I was finally feeling healthy enough to take up Motocross again. I had raced back in high school, but my injuries from the car accident prevented me from competing for almost 10 years. I enjoyed being on the road, traveling to races with fellow racers, and the thrill of competition. One day, I was out practice riding, hitting jumps and throwing my hands and legs in the air. I went off a 10-foot jump and threw my right leg up in the air. When I came back down, I didn't quite get my foot back onto the foot peg. I didn't fall, but my foot hit the ground the same time as my wheels did, and my leg bent outwards like a swinging door. I felt the worst pain I had ever felt in my life. There were two things I was deathly afraid of when I was playing football—hurting my back and blowing out my knee. Now I had done both.

A doctor's visit the next day confirmed I had torn my ACL, and I was on my way to the first of 10 surgeries I would have over the following five years to try and repair the damage from this injury. I am one of those people who grows massive amounts of scar tissue, so it seemed like every time the hair on my leg grew back it was time to have another surgery. I was fortunate enough to be connected with a physical therapist who played high school and college football and shared my athlete's mindset. He encouraged me not to get down on myself or about my circumstances. In one session, he was pushing me really hard, and I felt like I was at my limit. All of a sudden I came to the realization that the only way I could truly have strength to go on was through my faith. It was like God spoke to me and told me that no matter what happened to me, He had a plan for me and wouldn't give me more than I could handle (though at times, I'll admit, I wondered if he was testing the limits of that promise).

Because of my scar tissue, I had to work so much harder than the "average" ACL patient—but I was always up for the challenge. Whatever doesn't kill you makes you stronger, right? I just had a competitive attitude that propelled me to work as hard as I could to get better. Even though I had gained about 45 pounds and struggled at times with mild depression, I was filled with the faith I needed to do whatever it took to move forward. I refused to let myself end up like so many people—becoming a victim of their circumstances and letting life's challenges lead them down a road of bad choices. I leaned more on my faith in the Lord and the Bible, drawing strength from passages like Romans 5:3-4: "We rejoice in our sufferings, knowing that suffering produces endurance, and endurance produces character, and character produces hope."

Even after all of my hard work in therapy, my leg could only bend about 20 degrees, so my doctor decided to send me to a different orthopedic surgeon. This surgeon's plan was to go in and remove scar tissue to get more range of motion back. When I woke up from that surgery, I thought I would be "fixed," but I found out that I still only had 75 degrees of flexion. The doctor assured me that it would get better with time and therapy, but I knew I had my work cut out for me. Again, I was going to do whatever I had to in order to get better. I was going to physical therapy four times a week, fighting through the pain, and doing everything I could to distract myself. I was honestly living in a state of denial, but I had to be conscious of what I was doing so as not to hurt myself—there was a fine line between working hard and doing something I shouldn't do. I knew I had to keep my leg moving because that was the only thing that would keep that scar tissue from taking hold.

Over time, we made the decision that I wasn't getting the results that the doctor wanted, so the plan was to go back in with a more aggressive approach to the clean out. During that procedure, the graft that was in my knee was ruined, so he had to reconstruct the knee for a second time. I was released to go home and started therapy...again. But this time in therapy, I was having significantly more pain than before, and my leg was really swollen and hot. One day, when I tried to bend my knee a little further than it wanted to go, all of a sudden a little pinhole opened up and fluid started shooting out! I went back to my doctor and he drained my knee and told me to go home and rest. About 1:00 a.m. that night, I woke up in terrible pain and my knee was the size of a volleyball. I went straight to the hospital, and underwent emergency surgery for what turned out to be a staph infection. Because of the infection, they had to take everything out of the joint and reconstruct it for a third time.

At this point, I felt pretty beat down. There were times where I literally felt like I was dying (the doctors later told me that I actually did almost die at one point). Even though the hits just kept on coming, I knew I had to keep moving forward, keep fighting, and keep giving my body a chance to heal. I was released two weeks later and sent home with IV antibiotics. I eventually healed from the infection and started back to therapy once again.

Over the next few years, I continued to have surgeries to remove scar tissue. There was talk of doing a knee replacement, but I was too young and I wasn't really at the point where I "had to" do it. The surgeons decided that they didn't want to keep cutting my knee open, so after 10 surgeries over a five-year period, they told me I just needed to do physical therapy and it would loosen up. I worked hard, and slowly but surely, I did get better, but I had to learn how to do things differently. I had to teach myself to walk all over again, and it required great discipline to know when to rest and not push myself too much. All I had known in my life was to just bull my way through everything. Those who know me have often compared me to a machine—I only know one speed, and that's "ON"—so having to slow down and think more about what I was doing was a huge adjustment.

During my time in therapy, I saw many people come in struggling with some of the same surgeries I had been through and not handling it very well. I met several people I would call "complainers." It showed me what I don't want to be, and gave me more strength because I knew I didn't want to go down that road. God made me a different person with the strength and the faith He gave me – I was filled with the sheer will to go on in the face of adversity and live my life with purpose. People go through all kinds of struggles in life, mine just happened to be health issues; and no matter how bad things were for me, I knew there was always someone who had it worse. At the time, I really felt like I was supposed to help people, and I did that by talking to people when I was at my physical therapy appointments. Other patients would tell me that I was an inspiration to them. I knew I was growing through my struggles, and that's what life is all about.

As I got better, I was able to start doing some of the things that I used to do, like snow skiing (with a knee brace, of course), but again I wasn't able to do what I really loved – race motocross. Like football, it was something I had to put behind me. Through all of this, I knew that God had plans for me. I just had to keep my head up and move forward. But what I struggled with was that I couldn't move forward like I wanted to. I always had to be conscious of what I was doing so I didn't hurt myself or set myself back. This was just a part of dealing with adversity. As big a part of my life as motocross had been, I couldn't let the fact that I had lost it and football be my focal point. I had to keep living my life. I was able to go back to work in construction, which really made me happy and gave me a sense of normality. Finally, my life didn't revolve so much around my knee and physical therapy. Work was a distraction, but a welcome one. I was still having pain and swelling, but I just dealt with it. I knew there was nothing else I could do, so it just became my normal.

A few years later, I started having pain in my hands—the worst pain was in my fingertips. When I would bump the ends of my fingers (which, when you are in construction, happens all the time), I would get this sharp electrical-type pain. After some testing and one exploratory procedure, I was diagnosed with Psoriatic Arthritis, an autoimmune disease that attacks the joints. I tried taking several different medications, but the medicine itself made me deathly ill. I felt like I had one foot in the grave. It seemed like every time they messed with my immune system, I got sicker and sicker. This scared me again like my knee injury—it was that "pain that doesn't go away." I finally decided to just try and manage the condition with pain medicine, which worked fairly well for about the next 10 years.

During this time, I was blessed to have a son, Justin. Having him in my life motivated me to start going to church. Every week that I went I honestly felt like the pastor was talking about me, and the things that I was going through. It was like the message was written for me personally, because it so directly applied to my life. That is really what awakened my faith and reinforced what I had known all along—that God had a plan for me. I started praying more, and learning to talk to God like I was talking to a friend. I knew that I needed to just keep living my life in a positive way, and being a good reflection of his love so that His will could be done in me.

The low back pain from my car accident never completely went away, and as time went on, it started getting worse (most likely due to my arthritis). The pain was getting so bad that I couldn't think straight, and I was having trouble working. More body parts were starting to hurt, and I was battling fatigue worse than ever. The fatigue was the worst part because I felt so worn out—I had no energy. I was just miserable. I would have rather dealt with pain than the fatigue any day. On top of this, I was taking stronger and stronger pain medicine, always worried about the dangers that entailed.

One positive thing about not being able to work was that it enabled me to be more involved in my son's life and go to all of his football and baseball games. It was at one of those football games, when Justin was injured during a play, that I met my beautiful wife, Juli. She was the Athletic Trainer on the field for his game that day. As if I wasn't busy enough battling my Psoriatic Arthritis and orthopedic issues, I went and fell in love! We were married a year later on the beach in Carmel.

Only a year and a half into our marriage, I finally reached the point where I had to have my knee replaced. I knew that starting with surgeries again would be opening Pandora's box, but we were out of options. I had that surgery in March of 2011, followed by five more surgeries over the next two years to clean out scar tissue and release some of the nerves in my lower leg. To say this was a challenging time would be an understatement. Sometimes it felt like Groundhog's Day—every day the same thing over and over, never changing.

After I finally started to get better, my wife and I felt God was calling us to move back to Texas (where she was born), so we picked up everything and moved halfway across the country to start completely over. Having lived the majority of my life in Carmel, I'd had the same doctor since I was 18 years old. There was a level of security and trust with him, knowing I could call and he would fit me in, if not right when I called, at worst the next day. When we decided to move, I had no choice but to find a new doctor. You ask around, you do your homework, you do research online, but you never really know what you are going to find. I thought my first doctor was a blessing, but he turned out to be more of a challenge. At times, I wondered if he had even read my chart. After about a year, we finally parted ways, which ended up being a blessing in disguise because the doctor I have now is such a great fit for me. She understands me and works with me based on the ups and down of my condition. For me, I don't want just a doctor, I am really looking for more of a friend, because there has to be that mutual trust where I know that they are doing their due diligence to really learn about my condition and what does and doesn't work for me.

Thanks to my wife's connections with her new chiropractic practice and her knowledge in chiropractic and nutrition, I was able to find the proper supplements to help with some of my main symptoms like inflammation and nutrient imbalance. But what has helped me the most was having my DNA tested, which showed me exactly what my body was doing, what I need (and more importantly don't need!) to be taking and doing. It showed what kind of exercise I responded best to, and I acted accordingly. Contrary to popular belief, there is no "magic pill" for anything, but thanks to my wife, despite continuing to battle my Psoriatic Arthritis, I am the healthiest I have been in my whole life. Because she shares the same level of faith as me, she has not only helped me physically, but also spiritually as we walk the same walk.

After everything I had been through with my knee, I didn't think things could get any worse than the first 10 surgeries in five years or the next six surgeries in two years. But just when I thought I had everything figured out and thought I had been through the worst of times, it turned out to be just the beginning. Yes, the hits just kept on coming… Within the first year of moving to Texas, I had three dental surgeries, tore my rotator cuff and had that repaired, and then faced the biggest challenge of my life—my neck surgeries. I woke up one morning feeling like I had broken my neck. It was the scariest pain of my life because I couldn't move and the pain was so intense. For the first time in my life, I truly felt what it was like to panic and to feel the anxiety of not knowing what was going on. I contained myself enough to get downstairs and tell my wife what I was feeling, and she rushed me to the ER. A few days and several tests and scans later, I was having my first neck fusion surgery. Unfortunately, we would later come to find that my surgeon did not do a thorough job and had missed the main cause of my symptoms. I spent nine days in the hospital, and came home in a neck brace.

In the midst of all of this, my wife and I were knee-deep in the process of infertility treatments, trying desperately to have our first child together. By the grace of God, after several years of trying on our own and two failed procedures, we had a successful in-vitro fertilization (IVF) transfer in April of 2015. During this time, I also found a new spine surgeon who was extremely thorough and told me I would need not one, but two major surgeries to repair my neck. So, with my wife only 10 weeks pregnant, I checked in for what would end up being a three-week hospital stay after two neck procedures that lasted over six hours each.

To be honest, I don't even remember the first week after my surgeries. I was in and out of consciousness and in so much pain that it all seems a blur. As much medicine as I was on, I was in the worst pain of my life. It hurt so bad, I really wanted to die. For the first time, I was saying "I can't," and I was so mad at myself for doing that. It was the lowest point in my life - but I knew I couldn't give up! I knew I didn't want to turn into the person who says they can't do something. I just had to take that leap. I prayed to God that He would help me to just get out of bed. I found comfort in the sound of my wife's voice, softly singing to me as she watched me endure this horrific recovery. The thought of my child growing in her belly gave me the strength that I needed to press on. I was no longer living life for just for myself—it was about them. They needed me to be okay, and I was going to do whatever it took to get home. I needed to be stronger than ever. As I sat up for the first time, I felt like I could hear my high school football coach, "That's my Marine!" and it took me back to that athlete's mindset. Every single play, I played 100%. No matter what, I would just keep getting up. I had to turn into that machine again if I was going to get better and get back to my life. It was such a victory to me to overcome the incredible pain I was in, get out of bed, and stand up. That first step out of bed was my first step on the long road to recovery.

As I look back over all I've come through, in the back of my mind I always know that it's not over. I will continue to battle with my health for the rest of my life. Though I know that I may be faced with bigger challenges, I also know and have seen that each challenge allows me to find new strength I never knew I had. My journey has given me such a great depth of knowledge and experience, and I believe that sharing it with others can help give them the strength they need to overcome their own struggles and battle adversity. To me, it has never been as much about what happens to me as how I respond to what happens to me. I have learned that I CAN make it through anything, no matter what comes my way. Never giving up. Staying strong. Keeping the faith. There have been times I have just stopped and told myself to smile for no reason at all, and it would make me feel better. Sometimes a smile can be the best remedy. Through everything I have had to deal with and as bad as these things can be, this journey has brought me my greatest gift. It has enabled me, at 52 years old, to be a stay-at-home father to my beautiful daughter, Cadence, enjoying the happiest days of my life with her and her mother. Life is good. ∎

WES WESTCOTT *was born and raised in beautiful Carmel, California, where he spent 20 years in the construction business. An athlete at heart, Wes has played football, baseball, and golf, as well as enjoyed water and snow skiing, mountain biking, and racing motocross. After suffering multiple debilitating injuries, he has felt called to help encourage others with chronic pain issues to overcome their health challenges by sharing his experiences and his genuine faith, positivity, and hope. Wes enjoys cooking, music, fitness, nutrition, and photography, but his greatest joy is his family. He is blessed to be a stay-at-home father to his daughter, Cadence, and loving husband to his wife, Juli.*

CONTACT INFORMATION
weswestcott@yahoo.com

18

Perseverance - Never Give Up On Your Dream!

Michele Willburn

"You are an Iron Man!" I didn't hear that when I crossed the finish line, so I didn't really know if I had made it in time. The last few hours had been tough, and I wasn't sure if I was going to make the final cutoff.

Seventeen hours ago the cannon exploded, and we were all off swimming. Pandemonium would describe how it started. I waited a few minutes for all of the serious swimmers to get a head start. It was dog-eat-dog out there. Like me, most of the swimmers around me weren't the strongest swimmers. There was a lot of kicking. A couple of good kicks landed in my stomach. Someone even kicked off my goggles. "Swim! Swim! Swim!" That's what I kept thinking. And that's what I did!

The swim portion of an Iron Man triathlon can last up to two hours and 20 minutes. If you finish after that, you're pulled out of the race, disqualified. I finished and was on the timing mat at two hours and 15 minutes. First cutoff of the day: accomplished!

The 112-mile bike ride was next. As soon as I got on my bike, I realized I was missing my heart-rate monitor. I trained knowing where my heart rate needed to stay. If I let it go too high too soon, I would bonk, and likely not be able to continue after the bike ride. I didn't have time to go back. I had done some riding using my perceived exertion instead of heart rate. It's not as accurate, but that would have to work today.

The next cutoff point was coming up 56 miles into the bike ride. Rolling into the water stop, a race official walked over and told me that I had less than five minutes to get back onto the course if I wanted to make the cutoff time. The volunteers at the bike water stops treat the athletes like a car in a pit stop. They assured the race official and me that I would be finished there in plenty of time. I stopped, didn't even get off my bike. The volunteers brought me water, snacks, and even applied sunscreen on me, and I was done in less than five minutes. On my way again… only 56 more miles left to ride today. I might be on the edge of disqualification, but I was still going strong!

The second part of the bike ride was tougher than the first half. My legs were starting to cramp. Was I getting enough electrolytes? It was pretty hot outside, but I felt like I was hydrating enough. The bike water stops provide plenty of water. Bike riders ride by and grab water bottles that the volunteers hand you. I don't have enough balance for that so I wear a camel back. It's not aerodynamic (a word that triathletes use all the time), but it keeps me hydrated and I can save time not stopping at all of the water stops. I got off my bike to stretch and took some additional salt pills to help with the cramps. Luckily, the salt pills worked and got me to the end of the 112-mile bike ride. Thank goodness that was done! Two volunteers met me at the bike finish to help me with my bike. As soon as I saw them I said, "I need the hell off this bike!" I was never so happy to be on my feet! Now I had to run 26.2 miles.

Time for the third and last part of the race…the marathon, 26.2 miles! As I was walking to the transition tent, I was met by another race official and informed of another cutoff. I had less than five minutes to get onto the run course or I would be disqualified. There was no time for any rest! The volunteers helped me tie my running shoes. I put on my running hat, and I was off. Three loops of about nine miles each, and I would be an Iron Man. That's all that was left now! I had done this many times before. This would be my 12th marathon. I love to run! I love the way it makes me feel. When I finish a marathon—no matter how long it takes—I feel so strong and powerful, like I can do anything! I had never run a marathon after riding 112 miles and swimming 2.4 miles first. It felt very different this time.

The marathon went slow. I had plenty of time for walking and running—six-and-a-half hours. My slowest marathon had taken six hours, when I was having some trouble with my back that day. This should be a piece of cake, right? I started walking more than running which really started slowing me down. After finishing the first two loops, I was getting tired both physically and mentally. It was past 9:30 p.m. I had been going at this over 14 hours. It was dark. I had never run a marathon at night before. Mentally, this was becoming very challenging. At one point, I almost got lost. I took a wrong turn because it was pitch dark and I couldn't see anything. Frantically, I yelled, "Where is everyone?!" A bunch of people started waving and yelling, and I ran that way. I had another cutoff point soon. I had to pass 17 miles by 9:45. That time was getting closer and I couldn't see the 17-mile marker. I couldn't even remember passing the 16-mile marker. I was panicking. I couldn't be disqualified after all this! Then I heard someone say my name. It was my friend, Arlene. She came out there to run with me. This was exactly what I needed! God sent an angel to help me, and she did! She would run up and get water, coke, pretzels, anything that would help me run. She even ran about three feet ahead of me. I would try to catch up to her so that I could hear what she was saying to me. Later, she apologized for running ahead of me and not right beside me. I laughed and said, "I knew what you were doing, and I'm glad you did it!" I made that cutoff. I never saw the 17-mile marker but no one ever came and told me to get off the course. Arlene ran with me and helped keep me going for almost nine miles. Only one more cutoff to go—the final one—the finish line.

Then, about three miles from the finish line, we saw another friend who was looking for me. As soon as Arlene saw EJ she told him, "I don't know if she's going to make it. She's walking a lot." Running seemed impossible anymore. As I was passing one of the spectators, he saw me struggling and walking. He looked down into my eyes and said, "You have a little over two miles to go and 30 minutes. WALK WITH A PURPOSE!" Thanks to purposeful walking, my friends running and talking me through the final miles, and lots of self-talk, I made it to the final turn, into the finish chute.

When I say self-talk, throughout the whole race I kept telling myself things like: "I feel great! I feel energized! Mind over matter! You fail mentally before you fail physically. Failing is mental! I've got plenty of gas in my tank to keep going physically. I AM SO STRONG!" If I said these things out loud, I thought I would be more likely to really believe them. I never let anything negative enter my head. I couldn't!!

Finally, it was time to turn the corner, run up the final chute, and over the finish line. I had to do this by myself. Arlene and EJ had to stay behind. Ironman will disqualify you if anyone goes into the final chute and over the finish line with you. The last thing I remember EJ saying was "Michele, you can't walk anymore, or you might not make it. You don't have enough time before the midnight cutoff." I couldn't go this far, and not make the final midnight cutoff. I had to finish in 17 hours! The plan is to be an Ironman today!!"

When I turned the corner, it was like I was running into a circus. Bright lights and people everywhere! I was on a mission. As much as I wanted to, I couldn't stop and give high fives to everyone with their hands out. I had to run! I was so close! I could see the clock in front of me. At one point, I saw a six turn to seven and I wasn't sure if that was the hour (16:59 to 17:00). I just ran.

Finally, I crossed the finish line. I stood there and waited for what seemed like forever. Before running over the finish line, I never heard "You are an Ironman!" Every finisher gets that. Where was everyone? Finally, some volunteers came over, congratulating me, "You're an Ironman!" Did they know that I may not have crossed the finish line in time? They must not have seen the clock. I didn't know what to think, except that I didn't know how much longer my legs would hold me up. When the volunteers asked how I was doing, I grabbed someone's shoulders, and my legs completely stopped working. Next thing I knew, I was being wheeled to the medic tent where I received an IV, massage, chicken soup, pretzels, water, etc. A blood sample was taken, and apparently, those last few hours I did become very dehydrated, even causing my creatinine numbers to get very high. Nothing that a three-day salt diet wouldn't fix.

About an hour later, the doctor came over to release me. I was feeling normal again, actually pretty good. Those IVs do miracles! She verified that yes, I finished in less than 17 hours and that I was an Ironman!!

I was the last Ironman finisher that night. In the triathlon world, that's a big accomplishment. I can put the 140.6 sticker on my car now! And to think, five years earlier I was learning to ride a bike. I wanted to try a triathlon. A little one would do. I just wanted to try it. I really wanted to finish a triathlon! After all, what was I afraid of?

When you think you can't do something, don't be afraid to try. You don't know what can be accomplished until you try!

Thirty years earlier, I had a brain tumor removed. Some of the side effects included double vision, equilibrium problems, loss of motor skills (mostly fine), and headaches. After well over a year, doctors diagnosed and removed the tumor. Once removed, everything improved dramatically. My equilibrium improved, my double vision disappeared, my motor skills improved, and the headaches practically disappeared. Amazing! One surgery and seven weeks of radiation, and my life took a 180-degree turn for the better.

A few symptoms remained, but they were minimal compared to before my surgery. During the time I had the tumor and they didn't know what it was, I had to teach myself to write with my non-dominant hand (right hand). The tumor affected those fine motor skills on the left side of my body and since no one could tell me what was going on, I secretly taught myself to write right handed. I was 17 years old and afraid that someone would see me and think I was playing, so I never told anyone what I was doing. I didn't understand anything that was happening, somehow trying to figure out an explanation to all these weird things going on with my body. Why couldn't I write anymore? Why couldn't I walk up or down stairs anymore without holding the handrail to keep myself from falling? Why did I see two of everything? Why does my head hurt so bad that I can't even pull myself out of bed sometimes, unknowingly causing the fluid in my brain to drain and make the pain even worse? I wanted some kind of explanation so badly. I knew I had to write for school so I did what I had to do. I never gained enough fine motor control to go back to predominantly using my left hand. I still write and do many other things right handed today. I still have challenges with my equilibrium (balance). My hair never completely grew back after the radiation. My attitude was, and always is, grateful. After all, this is all a very small price to pay for my life!!

Twenty-five years later, I wanted to try to do a triathlon. I had wanted to do this for a while. I had finished ten marathons and was tired of hearing myself say, "I can't do triathlons because I can't ride a bike." I hated hearing that! I could at least try! Nothing is impossible if you put your mind to it with a positive attitude.

Have you ever wanted to do something, had a dream, but weren't sure how to go about accomplishing it? That was me!

First things first. I needed to learn how to ride a bike! The bike ride is the biggest part of a triathlon so that had to be conquered. I had tried several times but not been able to ride a bike since I was a teenager. One Christmas a few months after my surgery, I went for a bike ride with a friend and almost immediately crashed, bumped my head, and forgot Christmas that year! I didn't remember anything about anything that day, including the bike crash. Apparently, I still had some issues with my equilibrium.

Learning to ride a bike again was going to be a challenge, and one that I was up to. I love a good challenge!

My brother-in-law helped me get started. He would run next to me and hold on to the bike—just like my grandfather did for me when I was six years old—until he finally let go. I think I rode the bike for about a block before I realized he wasn't holding on anymore. Success! Nothing was natural about riding a bike. I had to think about every little turn, every little bump in the road, every little obstacle. I still do. I had a boyfriend who would practice riding with me out at the park. I fell a lot. Many times, trapped under my bike after falling, he helped me up, over and over again. I have scars on one of my elbows from all of the falls. The scar on my other elbow is from running. I was actually hit by a car one day! Luckily, and by the grace of God, I am resilient, and have been able to keep going. Think positive 90:10. 90% attitude!

Finally, I was ready for that sprint triathlon. I had done my brick training. I could continually swim 500 meters in the pool. I could ride a bike now. That morning, the real triathletes laughed at my Walmart bike. They laughed at the kick-stand. I didn't know kick-stands weren't cool. They laughed at how big and heavy my bike was. I had no idea how much importance was put on aerodynamics. I was going to start and finish my sprint triathlon today!

Finally, I was last out of the water. I had finished my first open water swim. I was so nervous in the beginning that I started hyperventilating, but I was finally able to calm down and swim so that I could finish. While I was riding my bike, my chain came off. I didn't know how to put it back on. Luckily a police officer was close and helped me. Out of transition, the second time, no one told me which way to run so I ran to the finish line, ready to get my new timing chip for my run. The volunteer asked, "You just started running? You need to turn around and go the other way." I finished running my 5K. After I went over the finish line (for the second time) I received a standing ovation from everyone. Wow! I found out that's what they always do for the last place finisher of that specific race. I finished! Triathlon goal accomplished! That was a sprint triathlon. I am a marathon runner, and I like endurance training. Soon after that sprint and another one, I started thinking about longer triathlons. Now, that I knew I could do one, why couldn't I finish a full one—an Ironman?

I've learned a lot about my determination. I've always had it when it was needed; I just didn't always realize it. My best training buddy, Cathy, would tell people when they asked if she thought I would be able to finish the Ironman, "Michele's determination is going to get her to the finish line."

I can think back to so many other times when I was determined to accomplish something and didn't give up. Never give up on your dreams! Push through obstacles. Don't let anyone tell you that you can't accomplish something because you never know what you can do until you try, and who you will inspire and empower to do the same! People have told me that I can't do things. Thank goodness I'm hardheaded and don't usually listen to them. I would rather fail trying than fail by never trying. Failing is just part of the journey sometimes. I use those failures to learn and succeed the next time. Sometimes I succeed, sometimes I have to reroute, and sometimes rerouting turns out better than my original goal. God opens doors for us, and it's not always the door that we think it's going to be.

You don't have to be great to start, but you have to start to be great!

~ Zig Ziglar

MICHELE WILLBURN *has lived in the Dallas/Fort Worth area most of her life. Born in Fort Worth, she graduated with her BBA from the University of Texas Arlington. Later she became an RN and graduated from UTA again with her BSN. She currently works as a pharmaceutical analyst for a GPO. Michele loves being active, especially running. She may not be super fast but she has completed several marathons and loves the challenge of finishing a triathlon as well. Good health motivates her more than speed. Passionate about good health, and grateful for her own, Michele enjoys educating people about their own health, helping make a positive difference in peoples' lives. Michele is very determined to accomplish goals and loves motivating others to do the same. Tell her she can't do something and she'll probably try to prove you wrong. Delivering Meals on Wheels is something Michele has enjoyed for more than 10 years. For the past 11 years, Michele's favorite dachshund, Lexi, has been letting Michele think that she's the one in charge.*

CONTACT INFORMATION
michele.willburn@gmail.com

19

Coming Out of Darkness

Mary Wilson

Why am I here? I have asked myself that question many, many times. The answer.... I am here because a gambling man and an alcoholic woman fell in love a very long time ago. Is that who I am? Let's see.... I am a child of the sixties, the youngest of five, a child of abuse and blessings, a child who experienced the deaths of loved ones, a child who survived two traumatic accidents, one of which almost took my only sister's life.

Between the ages of six and fourteen my parents got a divorce, a strange woman moved into our house, a hurricane hit our town, I had witnessed a rape, lost my best friend to drunk driving, stopped dealing with life, started doping, found new friends, and found a new way of communication. I had found silence, fear, anger and mistrust a way of life. Now I felt accepted in the drug community and doping became my everything.

Again, why am I here? I am here because I decided to choose this, and not that. As a young adult, I decided to move to Dallas, to work for the SPCA of TX, to participate in my life, to have three jobs, to get clean, to cheat on my lover, and to lose my friends and my jobs. I decided to relapse, and no longer support my life.

This most certainly must be who I am. Why am I here? Over and over these words ran through my mind. Twenty five and homeless, I dug out of trash to eat, walked four to ten miles a day, slept about four to five hours a night, hitchhiked when possible, spoke to no one unless I was spoken to, earned about five hundred dollars a year, and had overwhelming thoughts of homicide and suicide. I didn't know how to find help, so I didn't try. I didn't see a problem. I didn't understand what had to change—maybe it was my fault, maybe I just didn't care. Is that who I am? With tears in my eyes the answer came back—NO. So, I found myself back in a city I knew well, because I was forgetting my right from my left, east from west and north from south. Days and nights began to blend together and I never knew what day or month it was. I was exhausted so I camped on the steps of a twelve-step group home and stayed in the area for the next three years. My old friends had nothing to do with me (a blessing in disguise) and my family heard from me on occasion (another blessing). I met a woman who pulled up a chair and began talking with me over the period of two to three weeks. After numerous questions, she asked if I saw a problem with my life. She must have asked three or four times as the weeks passed. I had answered no. I saw no problem with my life. Not too many people talked to me back then…so, I wondered what her deal was. What turned out to be the last time she asked the question, I said yes. Homelessness had become who I was. And that changed my life forever. I do know saying yes is why I am here.

She took me to the MHMR (Mental Health and Mental Retardation) county facility and I was able to schedule appointments to start seeing a doctor. She made sure I kept my appointments and that I took my meds. She kept up with me and my animals; she let me spend the night and let me shower at her place. After a few weeks of meds, I was able to contact my sister who sent me to two programs—Discovery and a seminar with Zig Ziglar. I didn't really understand everything but I participated in the exercises and felt like my life could go somewhere.

I continued to mooch all the self-help anyone was willing to give. I woke up early every day and was made to do something each day that equaled value. I talked about issues, formed opinions, saved money, looked others in the eye and spoke with them in conversations.

Then that question came back, why am I here? I fell out of line with my doctors and my meds. I stopped going to the county facility. Sleep was erratic and coffee and cigarettes were what I did with my day. I sold my truck—and still didn't see a problem. And again, I found myself on the streets—me, two cats and one dog. Everyone has a story. I wasn't ready to share mine until I saw a problem. As I journal I see where my mental wellness comes and goes. Even if I am not making sense I find myself writing as Gertrude Stein did. And so I submit to you, the reader, this portion of my upcoming book *A Journey, Chronicles of a Homeless Girl*.

May 3, 2016. So, I can't seem to move my paragraphs and it seemed to be the biggest battle for about ten minutes. I have been feeling suicidal all day. The past month has been not producing anything. I can't seem to out the parasites that keep feeding on my thoughts; just is what it is…which really is not an answer of any kind. The mowers are not properly working. Figured out the Toro and the screens won't come out of the windows in the trailer. Nails in the roof really should be replaced, and the clippers don't work. No one could sharpen them. There should be Bluetooth on this Dell windows system but I haven't seen it and I am doing something I haven't done in a long time—typing a journal and journaling correctly. The cursor just transferred to another line and I used to do that all the time. I don't want to use people and few, at least these few, won't be the only ones. Certain that's not well said…just as guilty.

May 5, 2016. Today and the past thirty days were supposed to be done and on with… I called MHMR (Mental Health and Mental Retardation) and left a message with the front desk—the name of the women raped in *Boys Don't Cry*. Who knows? Mom called, the weather is supposed to be bad again today and will probably fry this computer that's what they all say—lightning and all. So as a defense to this onslaught or tirade, I will remember to check in with case manager. They say that's a life bet. I love smoking. The offer to get high entered my life recently.

Just "no," then what? Listening to music "I'd Cherry". Please start work-ing. The two ladies from MHMR came out here and had me do a safety checklist. Just what do I do or how do I do it, when the noisy voices and thoughts get too much? I have a copy on my phone. I haven't been med compliant and that will change. I think the voices tell on me and sister loses it for it's not all about me. I miss Aunt Scottie. I have to feed the pups next door another day—enjoying it a lot. I haven't been able to do anything. I am sick over her being home tomorrow so I will try to not be in the house when she gets back. I know I over react but it won't stop in my head. Going over to feed the babies. Truly in terror over family com-ing home tomorrow.

May 8, 2016. It is three thirty in the morning and I need to sleep so I am not asleep when she gets back. We have heart worm—heard Stretch cough last night so I guess we all have it. We always have had it and it's where we come from—it's eventually who we are and the world killed brother with aids. I think sometimes that he died of heartworm so I have to remind myself that is the mental health issue saying that. I could talk myself into hating people, but maybe not. I need to start respecting others and not being so selfish but that's heartworm too. Sick over later today. So, lucky. Still have been freaking out a little and can't shake it. The medications help until I feel I am being poisoned by the people who love me. Have to hide my meds. It should not be a sudden realization, I am not stupid. My new phone and computer are great. "Janet's Throb" is on. If they have it their way it will be in one word or less. Journaling for me is helping, yet I cry over lost potential. Madonna's "Material World" is on. So I am afraid of her. I will have these things done when I get paid, and a ride. So unattractive. so helpless, aww. Helen Reddy's "Ruby Red Dress" is on. Still sick over this coming day and month. I've been told that I am scared or feel undeserving of the things I have and the monies I've received. So, beyond someone trying to take them from me I need to keep what I have—come either, or. Listening to Lisa Stansfield. About to turn the evil tuning box on...yak yak. Maybe the economy is trying to devalue itself.

May 9, 2016. Fell asleep for a while. It is ten am and I am certain the fear is a learned behavior. Among other stuff, a male voice got violent and then said I am in danger. Some time had passed between the two instances, much like it was when I was young. Tory Amos is on and all I can think about is Scotties' family being blamed and stolen. Sarcasm just ran through my head. Have to do the windows today maybe just the inside to get a head start on it. So, the mower's wheel wants to come off and we might take it somewhere to get it fixed. Or I won't be able to do that. I might try and retake the Murray back—it might have been used for parts. It's forgiven when there's no place to get help fixing mowers, but really two tractors and three walk behinds…it's an issue some people say that's being resourceful; having the mowers tore down and sold for scrap is resourceful. I just feel like there is so much to do and I have no ability to do it. If I hadn't been present at different times when these things were freaked on, I wouldn't think twice about it. I am grateful I see it as a problem that just stays a constant until something is done. In the meantime, they are patched together and preyed upon. Their just mowers. So, I have realized it is not about the mowers, it is about the feelings and the abilities, and that is what I am dealing with. These words were not found in a day so it will not take me a day to know what I need to know about how best to approach my mental wellness. Without all the murdering chaotic thoughts. Without all the dominant and submissive. I do the best that I can. These thoughts, although they are a part of it, I have to find a 'me' part and way of thinking that battles.

May 11, 2016. I feel much better today. The feeling of being sick was mostly old behavior, yet I was ready to do battle if called. I shared what happened the past few days and was rewarded with happy thoughts. I still feel I could do more if I knew more and had proper tools but I can't fight something that is already known or done. It is like wagging my tongue just to feel a breeze. In defense of myself, if I want to I can bring up the spending money on what is not working or even worse railing on another, to once again fix something for the ten-thousandth time or letting it be and seeing what the idea for the situation is. I prefer the latter. The house is coming along and I hope to have electricity by the end of May.

May 18, 2016. A few days or a day I haven't written and I've been drinking—not a lot, at least not what I consider a lot. I feel like I am doing it behind my roommate's back. Not really, just not wanting to drink with anyone. That puts me in a 'waiting for the other shoe to drop' state of mind. Electricians came out today and looked at a few things. Blessed. Maybe I feel guilty because I am not going to church. I mentioned a few times yesterday that I have a church I had been going to when on street but it was ignored. Not up to anyone to help me and I don't get all that involved, but anyway, watched a little on TV.

May 21, 2016. Woke at three am. It started raining about forty minutes ago. It is five thirty now. It is nice to hear the rain on the roof of the RV. I love my computer. I have something to do other than stare at myself with this neat little technology. Thank you, lady, gentleman and family for it. Teaching myself about a computer was the most maddening. It seemed I was always getting side-tracked and it was too easy for my computer to get corrupted and way too easy to lose time. Hours would go by and all I had done was internet—nothing productive. I hated it at first. Then I realized journaling was possible and filling out applications was possible. That was amazing, at least at the time I was impressed. Also, had a large glass of juice before bed. I am sure that is helping with added energy. Still amazes me this small computer holds as much space as my Presario did. Pawned that computer and bought another and pawned that one. It was just too much weight. Being on the street, carrying that was way too much, but at the time I truly thought I was going to get some kind of work. Instead, I was living day to day and found myself taken in by the whole deal. Never ending, needing to do this or that but always needing to get out of the way. Between taking care of us and possibly getting a trespass I pretty much had my hands full. And the liars—mostly security guards—would accuse me of solicitation and loitering which was the way of doing a job. But I am certain if the shoe were on the other foot they would beg and plead not to be ticketed. Seems to be the cool thing to do, when in reality it just keeps one anonymous in the bigger picture. In my opinion fewer people need to blend in and more people need to be seen and heard. I met up with Steph and Cindy and Debbie at the City of Denton Animal Shelter they were happy for me and my sis. We talked for about 10 min.

These are the journals of a homeless girl and should be kept in mind when reading. I am still not sure when the random thinking started or stopped. I know that through the diligence of family and friends I have been kept on task. Sometimes going as far as saying" that's a little out there Mary," or "Are you sure you have kept up with your medications?" has not been too absurd for me to hear. I realize every day I am growing and coming into focus more and more. As I have had to transcribe my journal onto Word Windows 10, I have found the typing class back in 1986 served me well. The skills are there somewhere, I just have to use them again. "Chronicles Of a Homeless Girl" is a true journey.

MARY WILSON. *My name is Mary Wilson, I live in Texas and have for the past seventeen years. During two periods in my life I was chronically homeless. The first period lasted ten or eleven years, the second was for three years. I have found many different ways of living in the forty-seven years I have been blessed to be on this Earth. My life has been so full of gratitude and love that I am overflowing. I have written a book of my journals and am continuing to write each day. I have learned that it helps me think. My family and my life have healed the many scars I have seen in myself through the years. Thoughts, although many times sporadic, can be what keeps us in the present.*

CONTACT INFORMATION
golfing1968.mw@gmail.com

www.ingramcontent.com/pod-product-compliance
Lightning Source LLC
Chambersburg PA
CBHW072237270326
41930CB00010B/2164